AMELIA EARHART

FINAL DAYS

New Evidence
The Images on the Reef
A Plane in Plain Sight

I found Amelia Earhart's Lockheed Electra by returning to the past and examining vintage aerial photos

by

Robert Grant Wealleans

This work, *Amelia Earhart: Final Days* is a work of non-fiction and speculation which relies upon historical evidence contained in various forms and media to support this writer's thesis about the ultimate fate of Amelia Earhart and Fred Noonan, on or after July 2, 1937, during their second attempt at circumnavigating the globe by air at the Equator, and in the days thereafter.

Cover photo is a colorized version of an unrestricted Library of Congress photo of Amelia Earhart created by *DonkeyHotey* and used pursuant to license terms.

Introduction

A somewhat lengthy introduction is necessary for all readers, whether familiar with the saga of Amelia Earhart or not. Since my work focuses on the past and discoveries made in that "past," it is necessary to establish in readers' minds a familiarity with events and historical circumstances from July 2, 1937 through 1945.

My motivation for writing this book comes from my fascination since adolescence with the story of Amelia Earhart. I was born in London, England. Like Amelia Earhart, my grandparents were also born in the 1890s. My Grandfather served in the front lines with the British Army during WWI and my father and his brother served in the RAF during WWII as ground crew and bomber crew, respectively.

Today, in my eighth decade of life, 63 years living in the USA, I'm a retired immigration attorney who spends his free time writing novels. This is my fourteenth book, and it is not a novel. The term "monograph" comes to mind from the Arthur Conan Doyle Sherlock Holmes stories wherein Holmes often wrote papers on identifying cigar ash and other exotic subjects useful for investigators of crime scenes.

However, I've no illusions because this work relies upon the discoveries made by other Earhart enthusiasts, history, and extant, historical records and photographs to support my two theses. I'm not writing a doctoral thesis. I choose to write in a relaxed, casual style. Many scenarios are repeated throughout the book but are there to keep those who know little about Earhart and Noonan fresh and up to date on what is known, what has been speculated about, and what I'm contributing.

This work discusses the fate of Amelia Earhart and Fred Noonan on July 2, 1937 and afterward, as the duo flew from Lae, Papua, New Guinea to Howland Island near the end of Earhart's quest to circumnavigate the world as close as possible to the Equator.

From Lae, the Howland Island flight-leg would be followed by a final flight-leg to Oahu in the Hawaiian Islands, and a final flight to California to complete what Amelia Earhart termed would be her last quest in a series of "firsts" for women pilots.

The duo disappeared on the most-dangerous leg of their quest—Lae to Howland—vanishing into the Pacific somewhere "near" their destination of Howland Island.

Historically, there are many aircraft and ships still missing. You may be surprised to learn that many missing aircraft went down over land and still haven't been found. In those cases, it is the remoteness and the ruggedness of the terrain that precludes finding them especially when the location of the crash remains unknown. Nevertheless, these plane wrecks are found from time to time either on land (or in the sea) either by active search or by accident.

Most sleuthing for these missing planes and ships involves research. There is nothing wrong with being termed an "armchair detective" when in fact it is all one can do especially for an incident that took place over 80 years ago. Sometimes, it is not feasible to journey to an identified crash site for many reasons, safety being paramount.

In the matter of Amelia Earhart, Fred Noonan, and a certain Lockheed Electra 10E with registration number NR16020, the pilot and navigator officially declared lost or dead on July 18, 1937 "after crash-landing into the Pacific Ocean on July 2, 1937," there is a plethora of evidence that existed on, near, and after that date of her disappearance which says otherwise.

Many of you are thoroughly familiar with every theory, "fact," and circumstance of Amelia Earhart's final flight and ultimate demise as put forth by many authors these past eighty-three years. What prompted this contribution by me are the very recent discoveries I made in two aerial photographs taken in 1941 and 1942, and a subsequent, but extremely important discovery in an aerial photo taken on December 1, 1938, of the same shipwrecked ship, the *SS Norwich City*. That 1929 shipwreck, what is left of it today, is aground the reef on Nikumaroro, formerly Gardner Island, located in the nation of Kiribati (Phoenix Islands). The two images that follow are a recent aerial view and a map of the atoll.

Note that the remains of the Norwich City are still visible on the edge of the reef at the waterline in the lower right of the photo (arrow) near the lagoon entrance. The lagoon is a mile wide at its widest point. The slightly submerged coral reef that forms a perimeter of some ten kilometers is notable.

Below (next page) is a map of the atoll for your reference. The arrow points to the reef edge where the remains of the shipwrecked Norwich City still can be seen, and where I hope to prove to you that Amelia Earhart used this reef area at low tide to execute an emergency landing on July 2, 1937. I also invite you to view Nikumaroro using Google Earth.

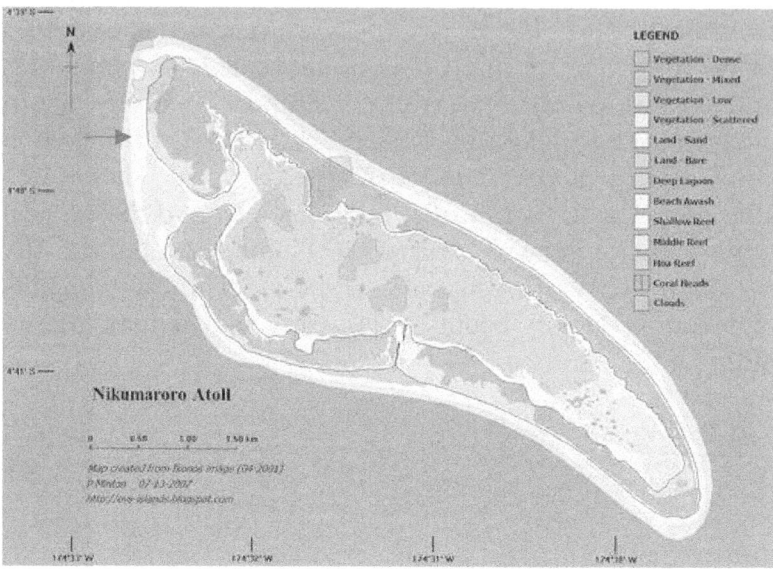

Aerial views of the aground *SS Norwich City* taken in June 1941 and January 1942 follow:

Apologies for the blurriness in the latter, January 1942 photo but the camera obviously jiggled or moved as the photo was taken. Remember that these black and white photographs were taken probably by using a handheld camera from the observer's seat in a biplane. Yet, those photos hold valuable images which I discovered in August 2019 while Robert Ballard was exploring this very island and looking for Amelia Earhart's Lockheed Electra aircraft (or any identifiable piece of that plane).

Unfortunately, (due to uploading & publisher processing) the reproduction of these photos in the paperback version of my book is not of the best quality. Therefore, I offer the reader better quality photos at my go-daddy site at:

https://robertgrantwealleans-author.godaddysites.com/

From the limited feedback for my publication of this work and the new information I've discovered, both positive and negative, it occurs to me that possibly no one has ever noticed these aforementioned "hidden" photographic details before or published their findings assuming they had noticed what I discovered. We will revisit these photos in depth in a later chapter. They do reveal a distinctive aircraft on the reef. I ask for your patience.

Other than my interpretations herein, what I discovered in these vintage, aerial photographs is the "new evidence" offered in this saga of solving the "mystery" of Amelia Earhart's disappearance. I believe it is a quite a *series* of discoveries which helps to explain the possible fate of the Electra aircraft and where it is probably located today. These discoveries that I have made may possibly explain why famed oceanographer Robert Ballard, discoverer of *Titanic* and *Bismarck*, found not one scrap of aircraft aluminum in, on, and around the reef at Nikumaroro Island in the 2019 National Geographic Special, "Expedition Amelia."

After I present this new photographic evidence later in this work, I shall offer a new suggestion regarding the fate of Earhart and Noonan which will tie together two, possibly three opposing schools of thought or "hypotheses" as to the fates of the famous duo.

As to Earhart's and Noonan's fates, in very general terms, there are proponents of a scenario that Earhart was actually on a spy mission. As the hypothesis goes, the Howland Island flight was a blind such that Earhart could secretly fly over and reconnoiter various Japanese bases such as Mili Atoll. But she crashed-landed in the ocean and was picked up and imprisoned by the Japanese.

Another similar scenario has her on Saipan by different means; another theory states that she crashed the Electra in the jungles on New Guinea after turning back toward the Gilbert Islands when she was unable to locate Howland Island on July 2, 1937.

Yet another scenario has Amelia Earhart landing the Electra on an uninhabited island, on the exposed reef there at low tide, and thereafter perishing there along with Fred Noonan as castaways.

Supporters of each scenario point to "evidence" supporting their claims. I put the word evidence in quotes because each scenario is supported by what proponents claim is the truth and which some authors claim is irrefutable. But unsworn statements or repeated remarks alleged to have been made by famous people are not evidence in the strictest definition and legal sense nor is a strong belief in one's own honesty necessarily a guarantee that the accompanying beliefs and conclusions presented to a reader are equally trustworthy.

True, we are not in a courtroom, but let a simple example reveal my thinking to you. Imagine your home surrounded by a fresh snowfall of a few inches. There's a package on your porch and a set of footprints leading to and from the package. It's still snowing, and those footprints will soon be erased.

This law school gem used to be about a milkman but let's say it was the mailperson. Did we see the mailperson deliver the package? No. What *evidence* do we have that he or she did deliver it? The package on the porch is obvious for one, and the two sets of footprints arriving and leaving our porch area is another. Male or female delivery person? What time did the delivery take place?

Absent the email reminder, we can speculate and judge by how eroded the footprints appear to be by the fresh snow falling. Here, do we assume a steady snowfall? Did the package get placed or tossed onto the porch? I think you see where I'm going here. Certain facts allow us to make inferences, reasonable inferences, and can allow us some speculation room for other detail and information we deem important. Just remember that in law, in the courts, an evidentiary web woven from strictly circumstantial evidence can be so elaborate, tight, and conclusive as to rise to the level of probative evidence.

That is, provided one believes that circumstantial evidence or finds it credible.

These various hypotheses about the fates of Earhart and Noonan are certainly interesting, though. I think I have found a common thread that unites them. An enticing and exciting possibility which I will develop strictly to give each hypothesis a fair examination.

Likewise, my beliefs and interpretations of photos herein welcome your constructive criticism though I hope they in fact stimulate you and others to further pursue and to develop what I have discovered.

A term that has been used pejoratively by champions of a particular scenario is to point to a conflicting scenario and assert "confirmation bias." This term means that a supporter of a scenario or theory or position will only look at and add what they consider is evidence to support their version of things. It is also what a belief in something will do to a person who only seeks events or facts that support their belief.

Unfortunately, these same proponents also believe that they have engaged in critical thinking where their position is concerned while others who oppose them have not. What troubles me is the vehemence expressed toward opposing views by certain individuals that extends beyond the subject matter and amounts to personal attacks on the character and motives of those who hold opposing viewpoints.

In response to my posted photos and hypothesis, one such author posted his reply that my "...conclusions were absurd and to take my fish wrapper elsewhere." The object in the photos was not addressed but was summarily dismissed by him—a proponent of the Japanese capturing and executing Earhart.

Another author, a person considered to be the "expert" on Amelia Earhart, shut down the thread and discussion on the group's website, dismissing the photos as illusions and the equivalent of seeing shapes in clouds. Yet, that same person (Richard Gillespie of TIGHAR organization) spent much money to enhance a small section of a 1937 photo to turn it into a landing wheel of a Lockheed Electra – a photo taken just 500 meters away from the port side of the shipwrecked *Norwich City*, and reproduced here:

Jeff Glickman

Enhanced by Jeff Glickman, the TIGHAR image does appear to show the distinctive Y-shaped wheel yoke, tire, and other mechanisms familiar to the landing wheel of a Lockheed Electra which many experts concur in. However, my photo discoveries and my hypothesis were dismissed outright though some TIGHAR members did indicate that filters thrown onto the photos I produced demonstrated that the object therein was no illusion. Gillespie didn't listen. Suddenly to my bewilderment, the major proponents of Earhart's and Noonan's fates close ranks and shun my evidence?! Why? I'll let you judge for yourselves. I believe they are embarrassed and loath to admit that they didn't properly search these old photographic images like I have.

Bluntly put, if you believe in the enhanced one-millimeter portion of a photo from 1937 showing an Electra landing wheel on the reef (Bevington object photo above) as being true, then it reasonably follows that the rest of the airplane or parts thereof may also be on the reef in other photographs, particularly aerial photos. In particular, this underlined enlargement of a June 1941 aerial photo of the stern and starboard areas of the shipwrecked Norwich City—a photo presented to you a few pages ago.

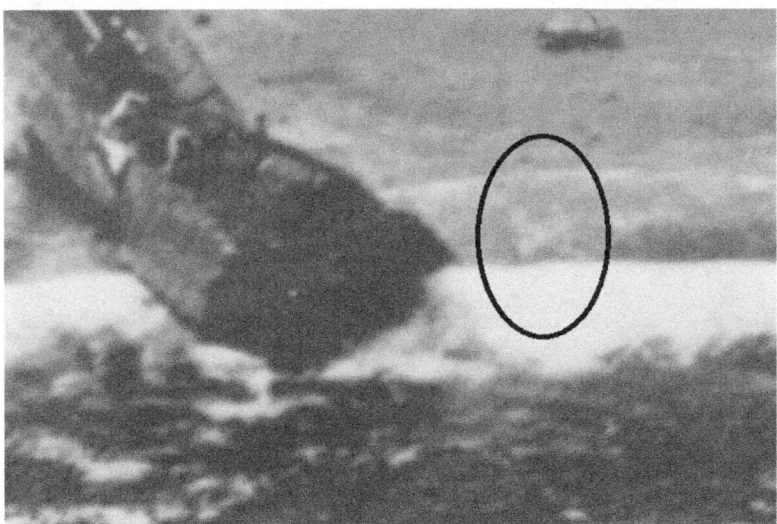

My discovery of this "ghostly" image (aluminum, partially submerged) appears to be most of an airplane that is strikingly similar to Earhart's Electra complete with nose hatch detached (front, nose hole), cockpit windows, port nacelle or firewall circular shadow, and wing stubs. Yet, it has been shouted down, ridiculed, and ignored. You will learn some of the reasons posited by opponents and why they oppose as you read further.

Let me add a similar perspective of this famous object and aircraft while it undergoes repairs in April of 1937. Remembering this and other photos from Lockheed is what allowed me to spot this near-hidden detail in the shipwreck photo above (possibly on next page).

Note starboard wing extension is gone but large engine firewall is present (removed on port wing). With the nose hatch removed, isn't this view of Earhart's Electra highly similar to what is in the shallow water next to the shipwrecked *Norwich City*?

However, unlike the enthusiasm and discovery quest performed on a one mm section of a 1937 photo to determine what was sticking up out of the water, my observations were dismissed outright, ridiculed, and hostility rampant! It smacked of ultra-religious zealotry and warned me that something more than scholarly debate was operating. Ego and money.

That opposition to new discoveries and ideas which I have encountered with my discoveries and opinions is not science, but it is politics. It is also hubris or pride, especially for one individual who has "controlled the narrative" of Amelia Earhart for over three decades while raising and spending millions of dollars in that pursuit of Earhart and the "Nikumaroro hypothesis" including taking an annual salary of approximately $167,000 to run an organization that has yet to find one historical aircraft. I do admire determination. However, I do not admire a determined effort to suppress ideas and discoveries not his own, and his outright refusal to even consider or to explore them. Ric Gillespie told one member not to waste time on studying the origins of a sextant box found on Nikumaroro. That individual persevered, ignoring Gillespie, and eventually proved the sextant box to be an artifact from another expedition, lost (misplaced) and left on Nikumaroro, and not Fred Noonan's sextant box.

I'm not going to delve any further here into that "mess" of conflicting opinions and hypotheses (though I will mention one further incident) other than to mention it in this introduction for the purpose of providing information and opinion to those of you not so familiar with the controversies and polarization of viewpoints regarding Amelia Earhart's and Fred Noonan's decisions on July 2, 1937 and their ultimate, speculative fates. The pursuit of what happened to Amelia Earhart requires one to prepare for hostilities.

Furthermore, I will use the term "evidence" loosely in this narrative and it should be construed to mean what existed at the time in writings, reports, logs, photographs, newspapers, and transcripts. When I later explore a speculative possibility in this narrative, you will know that I'm speculating because I do clearly state that.

However, that speculation will be based upon my attempt to join two, possibly three competing scenarios about Earhart and Noonan into one hypothesis based on plausible facts that do strongly suggest a common link. And yes, it is a lot of conclusionary thinking based upon the objects in the photos, but I won't apologize for the paucity of evidence. Instead, I'm grateful that this additional evidence exists and that I can bring it to your attention.

For the purpose of my analysis of what happened on July 2, 1937 as Amelia Earhart was low on fuel over the Pacific, in addition to the aerial photos presented, I will limit that perspective to the evidence that existed a mere week after she disappeared or July 2 to July 9, 1937, and which evidence is partially contained in both a transcription of and the actual newspaper article that was printed on said date in Melbourne, Australia. To this, I will add the photographic discoveries I have made and evidence contained in certain documents held in the National Archives of the USA.

The handwritten transcript of a newspaper article which I rely upon is in the archives of Purdue University and the Putnam papers. The actual "microfilm" record of this edition of the Australian newspaper is available online. Links are provided within the narrative that follow. As to certain of those "links" I must apologize for their length but that is the internet. Those who read the eBook version can copy and paste; the paperback readers must painstakingly enter each letter and symbol in their browser windows.

Additionally, I will rely upon existing logs of ships and reports therefrom from personnel who were either involved in radio communication with the fliers, or in the active searches for Earhart and Noonan from July 2, 1937 and thereafter.

Nearly all of these documents are available online, particularly in the National Archives of the United States.

I want to avoid any lengthy pre-discussion of any of the myriad, established theories, speculation, and other distractions with a strict focus on "evidence" whether actual or hearsay that existed just after she disappeared, and up to and including 1942. And where following such evidence leads to logical and reasonable conclusions.

My first thesis as you will see is backed by many pieces of evidence. My second thesis uses evidence from the time to construct a speculative and alternate scenario to what happened to Earhart and Noonan after their Electra aircraft went down on July 2, 1937.

I will admit in this introduction that my opinion is that Earhart absolutely *did* land her Lockheed Electra on Gardner Island, now called Nikumaroro in the Kiribati Nation, on July 2, 1937. What clinches that opinion is my discovery of two images of her Electra on a reef captured in two aerial photographs (1941 and 1942), and a highly possible, consistent image in a third aerial photograph of Nikumaroro reef circa 1938. You saw the object in the water and its striking resemblance to the Electra undergoing repairs just a few pages ago.

Please do not stop reading this work if the previous statement contradicts your beliefs. I merely ask you to give what follows "fair play" because you will find a lot of what you believe to be true which I tie into my discoveries. In other words, I try to find support for other theories such as "Japanese capture" despite the crash-landing on Gardner / Nikumaroro island. I attempt to "get" from Nikumaroro to a Japanese prison through inference and the historic record.

There in those three vintage photos previously mentioned, sitting on the reef at Nikumaroro formerly Gardner Island, are the remains of her Lockheed Electra. They are easily missed or unnoticed (and have been for eight decades) as you will see. Go back to the beginning of this work and look at the two black and white aerial photos. Can you spot the Lockheed Electra in each?

Unless your eye is drawn to the image in the June 1941 photograph (itself an enlargement), and you are familiar with what the Electra 10E aircraft looks like during repairs, it is easily overlooked. Likewise, without knowing about the image in the June 1941 photograph, one would be hard pressed to recognize the image of the Lockheed Electra found in the January 1942 photograph taken some seven months later.

Please note that in the June 1941 photo, the large debris just a hundred feet or so away and above is the precise spot you will see in the January 1942 photo except the Electra wreckage has moved to it! I insert this statement here precisely for the purpose of defeating those who shout "illusion!" or who love to say *pareidolia*. Does an illusion move? An illusion that resembles the Electra undergoing repair at the Lockheed factory in 1937 in the following photo of Amelia Earhart smiling from the nose (nose hatch removed).

The photo of Amelia smiling from the nose hatch explains the large dark "hole" or shape in the front of the airplane object in the June 1941 and January 1942 aerial photos that also happen to have shadows above it that resemble the Electra's cockpit windows.

The third aerial photograph from 1938 (presented in a later chapter) captures, in an extremely blurry blowup, the distinctive "dog-face" nose of the Electra in the surf line complete with nose hole (hatch missing) and "eyes" or cockpit windows. Taken together as a "three-frame-movie," these three aerial photos document the tide-induced, relentless journey of Earhart's wrecked plane over an estimated distance of some 700 or more meters beginning approximately July 2 to July 7, 1937 (the last date of believed, credible post-crash radio signals) to January, 1942 which is the date that the last aerial photo was taken which shows the Electra wreckage off the *Norwich City* starboard bow.

In fact, add the very photo that Robert Ballard relied upon, a blow-up of a single millimeter of film that produces an image of "an Electra landing wheel," (Bevington 1937 photo) and you have a four-frame "movie" or sequence that documents an amazing, miraculous journey along the edge of the reef for 4.5 years as the Electra aircraft wreckage was pushed and pulled by the tides and waves an average of 18 inches or approximately fifty centimeters per day southward and eastward.

In recent years, the Amelia Earhart story, mainly the story of her disappearance and aftermath, has been added to and embellished by several authors. I shall remind you that today, there are two or three main schools of thought on her disappearance: one is that Amelia Earhart and her companion, Fred Noonan, made a forced landing in the Electra 10E aircraft on uninhabited Gardner Island (Nikumaroro) on July 2, 1937 and perished there as castaways.

The second and third hypotheses are that Earhart and Noonan crashed in the Pacific (or somewhere in the Marshall Islands or on New Guinea) and were taken prisoner by the Japanese, and were subsequently executed as spies. The theory that she crash-landed on Gardner or Nikumaroro is ridiculed, derided, and is an example of the hostility directed toward Ric Gillespie of TIGHAR, the theory's major proponent, which includes cries of fraud, made-up evidence, and other vilifying assaults.

I'll just let a mountain of circumstantial evidence which Robert Ballard said cannot be ignored and my photo discoveries speak for themselves that the

Nikumaroro hypothesis, the theory of Earhart's fate first proposed by Fred Hooven that Earhart landed on Gardner Island on July 2, 1937, is absolutely correct.

Bluntly put, Ric Gillespie and TIGHAR gave you an Electra landing wheel, and I give you most of the rest of her aircraft in the same place, the same atoll, and moving around in the tides and surf, circa 1938-1942.

If you are an aficionado of this subject, then you are familiar with these subject matters and these competing "theories." One other and rather outlandish theory (debunked) claimed that Amelia Earhart had survived and was living quietly in New Jersey as a housewife. I still recall hearing on my car radio this announcement that they would report if indeed "she was the famous missing aviatrix."

No.

In August 2019, while I was perusing vintage photographs looking for anything that might be Electra airplane wreckage, particularly photos from 1941 and 1942 that concern Amelia Earhart and her fate, I spotted something which had heretofore gone unnoticed by me despite having viewed the photo multiple times. Apparently, what I discovered has possibly eluded everyone's attention for nearly eighty years. Humorously, I think it is the ultimate in *hiding in "plane" sight.*

I could see why the object in the photos easily escaped attention because it is so light-colored and practically blends into the background. This is due to the aircraft being made of aluminum and being partially underwater. Furthermore, the photos are "busy" with lots of rusty debris and a huge hulking object that draws the eye which convincingly implies that everything in the photo on the reef is wreckage from said ship, *SS Norwich City*, wrecked in November 1929.

I spent hours looking for other examples of this and other photographs online and found the self-same object in the January 1942 photograph presented herein and then located some several hundred feet south and east from its location in the June 1941 photograph.

Seeing this movement of the Electra wreckage, and cognizant of a photographic object said to be an Electra landing wheel some 500-plus meters north and west of the shipwreck in an October 1937 photograph taken by Cadet Eric Bevington, I hunted online for more photos and found only one.

There, in the 1938 photo which I found, a very blurry Electra nose peers out from the surf line—on the opposite side—the port side—of the shipwreck in the 1941 photo!

How is that possible?

Assuming the Electra began this surf- and tide-induced journey after July 2, 1937 from a point some 500 meters north and west of the shipwreck in the vicinity of the Bevington photo object or Electra landing wheel, then in the 1938 photo it appears that the Electra has moved, and is there in the surf approximately halfway on its journey toward the shipwreck (and beyond) as evidenced by the later 1941 and 1942 photographs which show the Electra on the opposite side of the ship and continuing its relentless journey to some unknown point to the south and east on the island reef (due to its shape and orientation). My conjecture is that the plane ended up in the lagoon or lagoon entrance which is nearby and in line with the general debris flow.

My use of those compass directions is general and not specific due to the orientation of Gardner Island / Nikumaroro to the compass points (see map in previous pages). But taken together, the four photos (Bevington's and my discoveries) prove that the Electra wreckage has moved some 600-700 meters or more over the period from July, 1937 to January, 1942.

I will elaborate on these "discoveries" later in this work and once more reproduce the photos referenced with the Electra wreckage circled. It is quite stunning!

I attribute my luck in locating this object to my extreme nearsightedness which has been my lot since age ten, coincidentally after a bad bout with German Measles.

Although I have 20/20 with glasses, without any correction, my distance vision is so bad in each eye that what a normal-sighted person can see at 500 feet, I can only see at twenty feet. My prescription of 20/500 and 20/450 does have one silver lining; it enables me to do very close work, even at my advanced age, without glasses.

Ironically, if I wear my soft contact lenses, my vision improves to 20/20 and 20/15 but I require reading glasses to see close with those contacts! I'm sure many of you have a similar situation. I suppose that is why I spent my childhood and adolescence doing puzzles and making models which I did without eyeglasses by using my limited distance vision as close-up vision.

The older I got, the more models and scale models I built. These included building scale model radio-controlled aircraft in 1:6 scale including many military aircraft from the two world wars. Included in my hobby was building 1:4 scale, working models of the V-8 engine and the Pratt & Whitney "wasp" airplane engine—the latter similar to the twin engines in Amelia Earhart's Lockheed Electra.

I have also built a scale model of the Lockheed Electra that Earhart flew.

You can view my upload of a working, single wasp engine and a *kit-bashed* "double wasp" engine I made from two kits which I posted some sixteen years ago on YouTube at:

https://www.youtube.com/watch?v=Jc-FEb2LCvs

You might say that I have a great eye for detail (up close) especially for aircraft, tanks, and ships and, though I am 72 as of July 2022, I still possess most of my very excellent memory.

Allow me to disclose to readers that I joined TIGHAR at the invitation of Ric Gillespie in August 2019 by donating $25 and then I resigned in October 2019 after just a few weeks. The problem arose because I believed I was being mistreated in their so-called "forum" by its director, Richard (Ric) Gillespie. He ridiculed what I had posted and had discovered in those two aerial photos previously mentioned (I had not discovered the 1938 photo at the time) and which he dismissed outright as illusions, wishful thinking, and *pareidolia* which the director fully defined in a response post. That's basically seeing Elvis in the clouds!

My subsequent posts or rebuttals posted by me were met with line by line denials usually beginning with "I don't see...." As for those of you who have never heard the term *pareidolia*, it is a type of apophenia, which is a more generalized term for seeing patterns in random data (think shapes or faces in the clouds, Jesus's image in a burned potato chip or wood grain, and other things). All of which are brain-induced illusions of which I am very and thoroughly familiar. Some TIGHAR members supported me, but Ric shouted and then shut the thread down.

Well, so much for "fun" and joining an organization (TIGHAR) committed to the premise that "Earhart landed on Gardner Island or Nikumaroro" as it is now known.

I'm puzzled by that reaction because TIGHAR went to great lengths to analyze a 1937 photo and a one-millimeter part of it which, when enhanced, was identified as a landing wheel from a Lockheed Electra by experts. The location of said landing wheel is calculated to be some 500 meters or more north and west (port side) of the shipwrecked *Norwich City* on Nikumaroro. Knowing the importance of that analysis and find, I was sure that what I had discovered in two photos would be studied further but I was summarily dismissed, instead.

Then, for a simple mistake and misunderstood paraphrasing posted in what I assumed was an informal, website "forum," I was accused of "misrepresenting data" and warned that all my future posts would be subject to scrutiny for accuracy and, if found inaccurate, rejected outright. Gillespie also locked the Forum thread I had started with the posting the aerial photos herein with enlargements and explanations. So much for new ideas not his own.

Sensing the outright hostility, I sent the director, Ric Gillespie, an email and resigned because this organization, its agenda, regimented attitude of its director, and his seeming unwillingness to even consider or investigate the possibility that I am correct by examining one or two aerial photos, were not for me.

On the other hand, noteworthy is my contribution to the TIGHAR cause to find and to retrieve in future the lost aircraft that Glenn Miller perished in while in-flight over the English Channel in 1944. Who knows? In future, Glenn Miller's Norseman may become the *first* aircraft TIGHAR recovers in its several-decades existence as an organization.

Here is the background of the aforementioned contribution which I made and which led to Gillespie inviting me to join TIGHAR.

Before I joined TIGHAR at Gillespie's invitation, I discovered that the TIGHAR director Ric Gillespie had stated that the Norseman aircraft (Glenn Miller's plane lost in 1944 over English Channel) carried *no* parachutes. This I knew was incorrect. I remembered something from my plastic model-building days and, sure enough, a few minutes online search in the WW2 manual of said Norseman aircraft clearly described a "parachute-equipped emergency radio beacon" installed just forward of the port passenger door.

The existence and location of that parachute-equipped emergency radio on the Norseman aircraft suddenly became extremely important to TIGHAR Director Ric Gillespie because it was the one stumbling-block he admitted to that he found in a "fisherman's" description of an aircraft he had snagged in his nets in 1985 in the English Channel that had parachute cords streaming from an open cabin door.

That added description of parachute cords or static lines by the "fisherman" (as he is known and referred to by TIGHAR) plus his crude, hand-drawn sketch of a Norseman, hindered Gillespie's decision to go look for the plane despite having a set of antiquated coordinates (a defunct system) of where the "fisherman" released the plane back into the Channel.

This revelation in the form of my impromptu email to Gillespie, and his gratitude for my "contribution" (described by him to TIGHAR members as 'occult evidence') prompted him to suggest that I join TIGHAR which I did.

As the perhaps overly enthusiastic "new kid" on TIGHAR's forum, I believe I was wrongly criticized for daring to disturb their near three-decade search and accumulation of data on Amelia Earhart. There were a few comments to that effect that I was just another new member disturbing their findings made over thirty years ("as usual").

What I read in those comments and interpreted was that the organization has said the same things so many times that it has become gospel and indisputable to them much like Gillespie's erroneous statement that there were no parachutes aboard the Norseman aircraft in which Glenn Miller perished. He says a lot of other "gospels" such as "Earhart's plane slipped off the reef at Nikumaroro into the depths."

"Fiction and speculation. But repeat it often enough when you try to control the narrative about Earhart and people accept his "expert" view.

My photographic discoveries of Earhart's Electra were scoffed at by Gillespie and members of TIGHAR, and my theory concerning debris drift for the Electra fuselage was labeled as too incredible to believe since my critics could not imagine how something as large as the Electra escaped notice from both the visitors and later inhabitants of Gardner / Nikumaroro.

These critics forget about several things such as the tides and the distance from the inhabited camp to the shipwreck and beyond, and that it was taboo or off-limits to the natives or colonists by their British masters due to the human bones found there opposite the shipwreck and no doubt the remains of the disinterred sailors (from weathering or crabs) who had drowned during the grounding of the ship in 1929.

To me, this bizarre criticism of my discoveries was an amazing example of their not remembering their own discoveries and their publishing much anecdotal information on their website gleaned from natives who lived on Nikumaroro from 1938 to 1963. Such things as *the plane that you could see at low tide*; *aircraft parts washing up on the lagoon beaches and used to make implements*; and one native who said he found a Pratt & Whitney "wasp" airplane engine on the reef and which he took to another island. Gillespie even went there to

27

this other island to look for it only to discover that the US Navy had bulldozed the former base and the "wasp" engine is presumably buried under tons of coral debris.

Additionally, this part of the island of Nikumaroro where the shipwreck was located was across the lagoon channel from the village. The inhabitants rarely went to this part of the island, and it was off-limits to them.

As to why the airplane was not generally noticed, the reef and tides plus the debris from the shipwrecked *Norwich City* easily concealed the aircraft as evident in the aerial photos presented—hidden in plain sight are aluminum aircraft pieces that are not rusted. Moreover, after bones were discovered on the beach near the shipwreck (presumably from interred crew who had drowned in 1929), the British official on the island made the area off-limits.

In sum, the "anecdotal evidence" from natives who lived on the island of Nikumaroro until 1963 about finding airplane parts on the reef and on a beach in the lagoon, an airplane engine, and that an airplane was visible in the water at low tide begs the question: Were these "illusions" too?

TIGHAR hadn't and hasn't looked hard enough, or its director is reluctant to look further for whatever reason. Did no one do their homework as they failed to do with the (Glenn Miller) Norseman aircraft parachute-equipped radio beacon? TIGHAR appears to be more of an adventure club with a dozen expeditions to Nikumaroro to "find Amelia" and a narrative of Amelia Earhart strictly controlled by its director, Ric Gillespie, who pridefully points to "artifacts" like pots, freckle cream, makeup powder so thoroughly researched but which are nothing more than contaminated detritus from an island inhabited from 1938-1963 by other islands' natives, Europeans, and Americans, including European women.

The consistent repeating of this statement that the Electra "washed off the reef" during the three decades TIGHAR has pursued the truth about Earhart, and a blurry photo of a landing wheel certainly prompted Robert Ballard to hunt in this area or "target zone" off-reef and to find absolutely nothing—not one scrap of aircraft aluminum in the ocean.

As Ballard said when shown the enhanced photo of the Electra's landing wheel in the "Bevington photo" from October 1937, he now had a *starting point* to begin his meticulous search for Earhart's plane. At the end of his search, another expedition leader remarked, "At least we know where she isn't."

That is a short-sighted viewpoint. Remember Sherlock Holmes and that character's famous dicta? *Once you have eliminated everything, then what remains, no matter how improbable, must be the truth.* My point is that the lagoon at Nikumaroro has not been *completely* searched (not even by Ballard), and that is where what remains of her aircraft may be found in my opinion (or further south of the shipwreck). TIGHAR members who briefly dived there in the lagoon or lagoon channel do state that the lagoon inlet is choked with debris, and silt. Gillespie himself admitted to me that the silt in the lagoon made it impossible to see underwater while towing divers on the surface ("snorkeling").

Here below is the 1942 aerial photo of the Norwich City (the Electra's cockpit and nose section off its starboard bow facing the surf) without enlargement. The lagoon entrance beckons beyond, doesn't it? In fact, a huge section of the shipwreck's hull is on the beach at the entrance to the lagoon some 2,000 feet away, and across the other side of the lagoon, in later aerial photos from the 21st century.

The enlargement for reference, below or next page. Note nose hatch cover off and dark hole plus cockpit windows presented. Also note the shiny debris behind the aircraft nose, the swept back leading edge of what I believe is the tail (upside down, broken off and reversed).

For purposes of limited corroboration of my finds, I will later include my lifelong friend and high school classmate's (Patrick S.) opinion on the June 1941 photo. He's a former US Army Intelligence operative (Vietnam War) *and* photo analyst. His blunt assessment found later in this narrative will somewhat further my credibility on this matter.

For my photo discoveries, I welcome and invite the same treatment accorded the 1937 Bevington photo of a landing wheel and the thorough analysis applied to it for application to my photographic finds. The images I found are larger than a single millimeter, and do not require enhancement beyond simple enlargement! How *scientific* to merely *shout* at my discoveries, and even misuse *pareidolia*. But that term sounds impressive, and scientific, does it not?

To be fair, one member of TIGHAR attempted to support me by pointing out that his use of different filters on the photographic image I posted did indicate the object was not an illusion. I had done that as well using software designed to analyze photos. Apparently, this member was ignored because Gillespie shut down and locked the thread I had begun. Then came those censorship warnings that I mentioned before. This attitude spoke to some sort of fear of a financial interest or presumed authority questioned or jeopardized so, I just moved on.

By his own admission, Gillespie states that a lot of people hate his guts. I can see why. The man must realize that despite all the work and numerous field trips to Nikumaroro to search for evidence of Earhart, there is still the possibility that he and others in TIGHAR missed something. What kind of sloppy research work is failing to look in an airplane manual for *any* mention of a parachute? Especially when Gillespie himself admitted that he had posted that Norseman manual on the TIGHAR website.

And how does one tell at a glance that the airplane image I discovered in the aerial photo (and two others) is an illusion and the product of the brain's tendency to *pareidolia*, or random assimilation of unrelated pieces of data, without proper examination of said photo(s)? How easy for Gillespie to simply dictate that the images are illusions to keep all his theories and statements intact, and his ubiquity in maintaining his position as expert, spokesman, and *showman* in all things Amelia Earhart.

However, I simply don't understand Gillespie's motives when my discovery furthers or champions their organization's cause for the hypothesis that Amelia Earhart landed on Gardner Island or Nikumaroro in the Kiribati Nation as it is known today. My thought is that an open mind, a mind that has had many photos analyzed, would see the merits of having the images I spotted also thoroughly analyzed (if original photos or negatives could be found). Indeed, TIGHAR photos and descriptions posted online at their website do indicate (as of 1999) that original negative copies were being sought. Update? Their website is a jumbled jungle of "uncompleted *discoveries.*"

As for my life-long friend Patrick, Vietnam War veteran who worked in intelligence and photo analysis, I've known him for over 55 years, and he'd be the first to call BS on my analysis of the 1941 photo. I'm encouraged by his positive assessment of the photos and his support for my publishing this narrative.

Since I have resigned my TIGHAR membership, I am pursuing matters on my own. My disclosure to you is strictly that and to inform you that I have no TIGHAR agenda here. However, what I have discovered does support their position and Fred Hooven's original hypothesis as to Amelia Earhart crash landing the Electra on Gardner Island on July 2, 1937 simply because the wreckage of the Lockheed Electra 10E is visible in historic aerial photos taken of the shipwrecked *Norwich City* in three different years and in three different locations, 1938-1942.

Yet, aside from spotting the Electra's wreckage on the reef at Gardner / Nikumaroro, I have another and different idea as to her and Noonan's fate after she landed there. Everything I rely upon in this presentation comes from the time of the massive search and rescue operation for Earhart plus a few documents, photos, and statements made by soldiers about their experiences during World War II, and statements found in logs and reports of the 1937 search for the missing aviatrix.

Understand that I'm not going to throw a lot of stats and specifications at you in this work. I'm simply going to show you what I believe to be highly plausible, and which is based on facts, evidence (documents and newspaper accounts) and reports from various people and organizations involved in the search for Earhart in the weeks following her disappearance and up until the dates three aerial photos were taken of the same shipwreck in December 1938, June 1941, and January 1942. I'm speaking about reasonable inferences and reasonable speculation based upon circumstantial evidence in fair play to other hypotheses and theories about her disappearance. Beyond that timeframe or years mentioned, I do add some statements found in other works covering this subject which I found germane to my theses.

Still, my work has somewhat of an additional surprise waiting for you. I invite you to read and ponder what may have happened to this brave and adventurous woman and her companion. July 2, 1937 was truly the longest day in the lives of Amelia Earhart and Fred Noonan as they crossed the dateline traveling east to "relive" July 2nd again while engaged in a vain and fateful attempt to find tiny Howland Island.

The National Geographic and Robert Ballard expedition has just aired (October, 2019). I deliberately waited for the broadcast such that I could add to my narrative, accordingly. I was very hopeful for Ballard's success. Yet, his lack of success bolsters my theory, considerably.

It's the morning of October 21, 2019 and I'm publishing this as an eBook and paperback on Amazon, forthwith, in an effort to shed light on truth or to at least get such evidence into the hands of Robert Ballard. Doesn't that explorer deserve to consider *all* possible evidence?

Note that in the Kindle edition, you may touch the photos and expand them with your fingers. Usually, the photo will appear in its own window for your manipulation and enlargement. In the paperback edition, please do go to the websites listed and copy and paste the photo in your favorite photo software for your perusal and perhaps better view or use a magnifying glass.

Amelia Earhart was a brave and courageous woman who suffered a terrible fate along with the equally brave and courageous Fred Noonan. May they both rest in peace and may their true and ultimate fates become known in future.

Respectfully, I ask you to accompany me on our "armchair" search for what happened to Amelia Earhart, Fred Noonan, and a Lockheed Electra 10E bearing NR16020 on its wings and tail. Along the way, I will attempt to blend in the various theories that exist about her and Noonan's demise because proving her aircraft crashed-landed on Gardner/Nikumaroro does not preclude the possibility that they died *elsewhere*.

I'm entering the following during a revision on January 29, 2022. Some accuse me of bashing Ric Gillespie. I merely state the facts. Besides, the preceding is an introduction or overview. Why did I include the Gillespie matters? I did it to answer the question that everyone familiar with this quest asks of me: "What did TIGHAR or Ric Gillespie say about these aerial photos and your opinions?"

Pareidolia.... I'm shutting down this thread on our forum....Don't post any further pictures or I will remove them....

Judge the truth for yourself as you read on.

1

Brief Biography of Amelia Earhart

July 24, 1897 saw Amelia Earhart come into the world with well-to-do grandparents and parents. The future looked bright. However, financial difficulties ensued which, coupled with her father's excessive drinking, made life difficult and nomadic for a while. After her mother received her inheritance, she was able to provide young Amelia with a good education.

In 1918, during a visit to Toronto, Canada, Amelia decided to help care for wounded and recuperating WWI soldiers. At a Toronto airshow, she fell in love with airplanes and aviation. Later, back in Massachusetts, Amelia worked in a boarding house that assisted new immigrants to the United States. Post WWI, saw Earhart become only the sixteenth licensed female pilot and president or head of an all-female pilot group called "The 99s" which organization still exists today.

Amelia was soon hooked on aviation, and an impromptu stunt (discussed in National Geographic's "Destination Amelia") where she displayed her skills as a female pilot at an air show and captured the public's imagination.

As her piloting skills grew, so did her renown. In future years, she would be rubbing shoulders with other female aviators such as the legendary Pancho Barnes and competing in air races with several other notable female pilots.

Amelia was the first women to fly over the Atlantic Ocean—as a passenger! Still, despite not piloting the plane, this brought her fame. Subsequently, she flew solo across the Atlantic and became the first woman to do so after Charles Lindbergh's solo feat in 1927.

Newspapers dubbed her "Lady Lindy" which moniker she detested perhaps because the press at the time said she looked like Charles Lindbergh as opposed to her "duplication" of his 1927 solo flight (except she landed in Ireland due to bad weather and didn't make it to Paris).

Fame was rocketing Miss Earhart. She was extremely popular, and she was invited to speak, lecture, and tour. Earlier, a man had come to her assistance to help with her lecture tours and publicity. This man, interested in finding and promoting a female pilot chose Amelia Earhart because she was college-educated, a pilot, and had all the needed piloting skills and charisma required. This man would later propose (many times) and eventually became her husband.

This man was George Palmer Putnam, who was a publisher and considered the finest promoter in the 1930s. And promote her he did! Various sources state that theirs was an "open" marriage. The National Geographic special, "Destination Amelia" broadcast on October 20, 2019 spoke of a note that Earhart gave Putnam before they married wherein "the promise to obey" would be omitted in the ceremony. Thus, though married in a time when a husband dominated everything pertaining to his wife, Amelia Earhart kept her name and her independence.

Earhart was an adventurous type. Some say she was fearless; some say she was foolhardy, including other female aviators who concurred in this latter sentiment. Nevertheless, on one occasion, without ever having flown the plane beforehand, she got into the cockpit of an auto-gyro plane and set a new altitude record that exceeded 18,000 feet.

Earhart added to her "first woman" list of accomplishments in aviation by flying solo across the Atlantic and the continental United States; a solo flight from Hawaii to Oakland, California in approximately seventeen hours, and then subsequently flew solo to Mexico City from there setting yet another "record" for women aviators. Earhart further stayed in the news by competing in air races while under the capable, promotional wing of her husband, George Putnam.

For a thoroughly enjoyable and excellent award winning and *Emmy winning* documentary, I suggest you view Nick Sparks' *The Legend of Pancho Barnes and the Happy Bottom Riding Club* on Prime for a look at female aviation in Barnes's day and Earhart's.

Earhart wanted the best airplane for her feats of aviation, particularly her final feat of circumnavigating the globe, and the purchase from Lockheed of a new twin-engine, aluminum-skinned Electra 10E was her choice. Powered by the mighty Pratt & Whitney nine-cylinder *wasp* radial engines, the plane was an elegant beauty and Earhart loved to fly it. In 1936, as a final feat for a female aviatrix, Earhart decided to try to circumnavigate the globe by taking the longest route around the globe by flying near the Equator.

The previous record was 17,000 miles in length; Earhart's proposed route near the Equator would turn that into *in excess of 30,000 miles*.

To this end, Earhart even wrote to President Franklin Roosevelt for assistance in her then-planned east-to-west circumnavigation flight, requesting either assistance with aerial refueling over the Pacific or at Midway or some other island base. In the National Archives, this letter from Earhart has a penciled-in note presumably from FDR to his assistant to cooperate with or assist "Mrs. Putnam." Amelia Earhart and Eleanor Roosevelt, the President's wife, were good friends.

Go to the USA National Archives website and enter Amelia Earhart in the search box and scroll down through the many documents there. I will refer to some of these archive documents as you read because it is difficult to include photos of them in this book due to size and format.

This round the world flight to be performed in 1937 was to be her last "first" and a fitting end to a remarkable aviation career for a woman of her time. She was nearly forty years old and probably wanted to enjoy the home life. Also, there were no further spectacular achievements for her to accomplish as a woman pilot beyond this planned circumnavigation.

As originally planned, this flight would be westbound, commencing in Oakland, CA and flying to Hawaii, and then on to New Guinea via some island refueling spot as her letter to her presidential friend (FDR) requested.

Preparations were extensive as were modifications made to her Electra aircraft. The original plan included two companions for the flight: Fred Noonan formerly of Pan Am Airways and Harry Manning who was much more experienced and adept at radio operation than either Earhart or Noonan, especially in Morse Code.

In Oakland, at the commencement of her westbound circumnavigation attempt, Paul Mantz joined the trio and the four landed in Hawaii at the naval base. There, Mantz oversaw maintenance to the Electra while the trio went into Honolulu to relax and wait before beginning the next leg.

Routine maintenance requirements for the Electra forced Mantz to fly the Electra to Ford Island (Honolulu) in the middle of Pearl Harbor. And it was from this spot that the Electra, Earhart, and company would take off for the second leg of the round the world flight.

A few words here about Paul Mantz who extensively schooled Amelia Earhart on flying the Electra. He was an accomplished aviator who later teamed with Frank Tallman to form *TallMantz Productions* which helped Hollywood and filmmakers with airplane stunts.

In 1965, while filming *Flight of the Phoenix* starring Jimmy Stewart, the miracle plane created from a crashed aircraft that was the center of the story was flown by Mantz and crashed upon landing, killing him. Online on YouTube, you can see the terrible accident caused by the collapse of the tail boom upon landing which then caused the nose to dig in and cartwheel.

Mantz's partner, Frank Tallman, continued with the company (that's him flying planes in 1972's *The Great Waldo Pepper* starring Robert Redford) only to later perish when his own plane crashed into a mountainside near Trabuco Canyon, California during bad weather.

March 20, 1937 presented Amelia Earhart with a wet runway on Ford Island in Hawaii for her next westbound leg of her first attempted circumnavigation flight. As she throttled up the engines during takeoff, the Electra veered, and it is said that she over-corrected on one engine throttle such that one wing and one wheel lifted off the ground putting too much weight on the other wheel which broke off resulting in what was termed a "ground loop."

It is further alleged that Earhart did not like using the rudder controls for such corrections during takeoff.

Ground looping is an aviator's worst nightmare. Many early aircraft, especially those with landing wheels set close together like the famed Fokker Triplane *DR-1* which the Red Baron flew, were vulnerable to ground-looping and many early aircraft required assistants holding the wings of the aircraft, running alongside it, until the aircraft achieved enough takeoff speed or outran the assistants. Even the famous RAF *Spitfire* had this problem, especially when landing. The *Spitfire* was said to be "a lady in the air but a bitch on the ground."

As a result of the crash on Ford Island, the Electra was heavily damaged, and the circumnavigation attempt terminated (postponed). The plane was shipped back to Lockheed in California for extensive repairs.

It has been alleged that Earhart deliberately cracked up her plane. I think such an assertion is nonsense. Further assertions state this planned crack-up was a part of the "secret mission" for FDR and the U.S. Government to spy on the Japanese which has some plausibility if it was merely to ask Earhart and Noonan to note all Japanese ships and installations that she flew over. But to deliberately crash? It is nonsense.

Hearsay statements made to her mechanic then and on-scene which were reported by him during an interview when he was age 85, that Earhart asked him to keep quiet when the inspector came to investigate the accident because the mechanic stated to her that it was "no ground loop," are interesting but hardly worth dwelling on or relied upon for some substantive conclusion. To purposely crash a perfectly good airplane on takeoff which is full of highly flammable and explosive gasoline (of two different octanes) for some nefarious, clandestine spying purpose is a scenario beyond ludicrous.

As for the ground loop, did she make a mistake or commit pilot error? Probably. Lots of pilots do. Have you ever skidded in your car on a wet surface or on snow or ice, and overcorrected? Remember, this is a woman in 1937 in a society that didn't permit or tolerate women to do a lot of things which we take for granted today.

The truth is that it was not until the 1960s that women were able to apply for credit cards without relying upon their husband applying for same. In her time, Earhart reasonably feared that her pilot's license would be pulled, and that is no way to end a distinguished and remarkable flying career.

Note also that as recently as some sixty years ago, doctors routinely conferred with husbands regarding their wife's medical diagnoses and suggested treatments. And what about today? We're still one state short of an Equal Rights Amendment passing. Update: It passed, but the time limit for its passage was up in the early 1980s, and opponents are seizing on that to invalidate the ratification. Another obstacle for women. Even the late Ruth Bader Ginsburg, Justice of the US Supreme Court, believed it would be better to start a new amendment drive.

And, as of this revision, the pandemic-plagued world and the chaos within the USA is taking center-stage with much depression and sadness around the world for the large numbers of lives that continue to be lost and the growing ranks of the newly infected. Then, 1937 still saw the effects of the Great Depression, the aftermath of "Spanish flu," and the looming war clouds from Nazi Germany and the Japanese Empire.

In 2020 and beyond, women still get paid less for identical work performed by men, and the glass ceiling is still intact except for a few "skylights" attributable to legislation, and some very courageous and determined women. My mother was a single mom in Manhattan (NYC) in the late 50's and 1960's. I admired her. In 1937, Amelia Earhart was probably reasonably fearful of an inspector pulling her pilot's license and ending her dream to have one last public flight flying around the globe.

Is the criticism of Amelia Earhart mostly and just because she is a woman? I believe most of it is.

As a result of this takeoff accident on Ford Island, a very frightened and shaken Harry Manning quit the team and the around the world flight attempt. Subsequently, in her second attempt at the equatorial flight, there would be only two people in the cockpit, Earhart and Fred Noonan. Neither knew Morse code other than understanding a single, repeated letter, and neither was as experienced with radio as Manning. Manning also would have served as a secondary navigator had he been part of the crew.

The omission of a competent radioman on the resumed round the world flight was a fatal error. Furthermore, Earhart's lack of understanding of all limitations of her own radio and broadcast capabilities was a second fatal error.

Unfortunately, this crash and Manning quitting ultimately contributed to the disappearance of Earhart and Noonan and their failure to find tiny Howland Island on July 2, 1937 because Earhart could not hear the radio operators aboard the waiting *Itasca* on her radio though they could hear her. And because experienced radio operators claim she failed to follow established radio protocols and did not fully understand the limitations and capabilities of the radio installed on her aircraft. I wonder if her radio receiver was faulty or broken. Earhart had definite clues about radio problems when she was in Lae, New Guinea just before the final and fatal leg of her journey.

These conclusions about Earhart's radio incompetence are justified but must be tempered with knowledge of the problems with radio technology in those days. Just remember that radio did not get into aviation's cockpit until 1928 when the fledgling Pan American Airways was experimenting with its usefulness in their S-29 flying boat. That's a mere nine years prior to Earhart's and Noonan's final flight and disappearance. More on the state of the art in radio technology in 1937, later.

Below are photos of the crashed Electra on Ford Island after Earhart cracked up after ground-looping on a westbound takeoff and first attempt at circumnavigating the globe at the equator. Note the starboard, broken landing wheel lying on the runway by itself. Ironically, seven decades would pass until a small object sticking out of the water in a photo taken in 1937 by Cadet Eric Bevington on the remote Pacific atoll then known as Gardner Island would be analyzed and enhanced to reveal a broken-off landing wheel of a Lockheed Electra. Many experts concluded the image could only be the landing wheel from an Electra aircraft. How many Electra's were there in that area of the Pacific in 1937? One! NR16020, Earhart's Lockheed Electra 10E.

And another, closeup image: (possibly on following page)

Note the proximity of the large engine nacelle and firewall circle to the fuselage and cockpit (important when you see similar shadows on the aircraft reef image), the starboard (bent) engine tilt and the crushed, broken port landing strut and wheel.

With the weight of the Electra dragging and spinning on the runway after right-gear collapse, it is easy to see how these engines might become easily detached in a crash. Apparently, they did not detach here but certainly might detach if left to the surf and tides of let's say Gardner or Nikumaroro over a lengthy period of time.

The shadows of engine nacelle(s) or bare firewall in the Electra wreckage photos presented earlier and later (taken of the reef & *Norwich City*) may or may not be the still-attached wasp engines but are probably the bare firewall. Note that anecdotally, a native reported (and Gillespie heard) that he found a "wasp" engine on the reef at Nikumaroro and had it taken to another island for possible salvage. Gillespie had a look but said the engine (allegedly) is buried under tons of coral debris courtesy of the US Navy when they abandoned that island and bulldozed flat all traces of their habitation.

Then, in order to orient you for the upcoming Electra aircraft wreckage in the aerial photos I discovered, I ask you to consider and imagine the result of wave and water action during the four daily tides, tossing or dragging the plane on a reef with broken-off landing gear, and *that image* plus the photo above, thereby leaving only the empty engine nacelles after the Wasp engines break away or the engines themselves still attached after the cowlings have been torn away.

I ask you to note the "dog face" or long snout of the Electra nose which mimics looking at any modern jet aircraft nose on. Note also the hatch in the nose of the Electra is still intact but missing in the photos taken during the Electra's repair at Lockheed (presented later). That hole in the nose mimics the black spot on a jet's nose. Hence my use of the terms "nose hole" and "dog face."

I found three such images in those vintage aerial photos.

2

Second Flight Attempt

May 21, 1937 saw Earhart and Noonan take off from Oakland, CA in the repaired Electra flying eastbound. The change in direction for the global flight was due to a change in the seasons and the weather and prevailing wind conditions over the Pacific. Might their unfamiliarity with winds at that time of year have contributed to their navigational error? Fuel consumption was also a factor to be considered.

One of my favorites (see a previous and later photos) is Earhart's pose inside the open nose of the plane which incredibly, along with these below images of the fuselage minus full wings and engines, led me to identify the images I found in 1938, 1941, and 1942 aerial photographs which will be described in greater detail in a later chapter.

Below are photos of the Lockheed Electra undergoing repair. Note the large, open nose hole, the nose hatch not installed at this moment. Note the starboard, bare firewall (engine removed) which may account for the circular shadows visible in the Electra image in the photos I discovered.

Originally, Earhart had the Electra fitted with the latest radio equipment and a pioneering new directional finder that would eventually become the standard in all aircraft. This new device permitted direction finding *and*

simultaneous radio communication which was an important improvement over a two-step procedure that was then standard.

However, the manufacturer of the "old" equipment persuaded Earhart to switch back to his company's "reliable and proven" equipment rather than to rely upon something new on such a lengthy and important flight. Unfortunately, Earhart took that advice and had the new equipment removed. This was possibly another fatal error or contributing factor in her demise.

In my opinion and in the opinion of many others, had Earhart not changed her radio equipment, it is likely that she would have found and landed on tiny Howland Island and completed her journey to Oakland via Hawaii, successfully, with or without Manning. That is, barring any takeoff mishap at Howland which is barely 20 feet above sea level.

In an Amazon Prime show, *Across the Pacific*, a documentary about Pan Am (2020), they recount an event involving an S-29 flying boat designed by Igor Sikorsky on a flight in 1928 from Cuba to Key West that was Panama's first mail route in the Caribbean. The airline had been experimenting with radio and its use as a navigational tool using a primitive direction-finder considered state of the art at the time. The trouble was that the receiver in the aircraft had broken down and had been left behind. The result was that their radio operator on board the flying boat named *General Machado* could be clearly heard but there was no way to communicate with him since he had only a transmitter and no receiver.

The flight from Cuba to Key West was a mere ninety miles and yet due to cloudy and hazy conditions, the pilot got lost. Then, after failing to see land forty-five minutes beyond the short flight time, the pilot of the *General Machado* elected a left turn thinking they were east of Key West and possibly Florida.

At the base or airdrome in Key West, listening to their radio colleague broadcasting from the aircraft, and utilizing their direction finder, they knew the truth which was that the pilot had just made an error and was now flying into the vast Gulf of Mexico unaware that a wind from the east had blown the aircraft miles off course. The error ended up being 300 miles! They had no way to contact the aircraft. The flying boat crash-landed in the waters of the Gulf. One passenger drowned, and the rest were rescued by a passing ship.

Does this sound familiar to those of you familiar with the Amelia Earhart saga? Earhart couldn't hear the radiomen of *Itasca,* the US Coast Guard ship waiting at Howland Island, though they could hear her. Earhart also broke several radio protocols that did not help her dire situation. Nine years earlier when radios in planes were in their infancy, if a ninety-mile flight had a navigational error of 300 miles and a fatal crash, then what about Earhart's flight from Lae over 4,000 kilometers or over 2,500 miles to a half-mile long atoll called Howland where she had no effective radio communication with the waiting Coast Guard ship, *Itasca*? It is not a stretch to conclude that Noonan made a navigational error for whatever reason, and possibly Earhart turned the wrong way thinking she was actually north of Howland Island instead of south.

But some "experts" simply refuse to believe it possible that the duo made an error of some 350 nautical miles. I point to the photo of Earhart's Electra on the reef which, if you believe that is her airplane, implies that something had to have gone wrong in their navigation. Yet, I am then challenged to prove how they flew to Gardner or Nikumaroro. The aircraft visible on the reef is proof enough simply by inference if you accept that the image is that of a Lockheed Electra.

Such is the nature of the opinions of so-called experts who need to admit that their speculations, heretofore, have been wrong but who continue to stubbornly challenge any new evidence if it contradicts their beliefs and long held and published opinions. In science, this is exactly what happens as new evidence and studies suggest alternatives to long-standing beliefs. I'm patient and confident that I will prevail.

Let's get back to the second flight attempt, eastbound. In Miami, during a stopover on the second attempted and now <u>eastbound,</u> round the world flight, for some unknown reason, a modification was made to the Electra. The rear starboard window forward of the rest room was covered with an aluminum patch. The National Geographic special stated that this was due to an airplane window cracking upon landing in Miami.

During an expedition to Nikumaroro (formerly Gardner Island) by members of TIGHAR in the 1990s, an aluminum piece full of rivet holes and one remaining rivet was uncovered. It had a wire attached (a feature ignored for quite a while). The piece of aluminum does not match nor do the rivet holes line up with any piece of aluminum on existing, vintage Electra 10 aircraft or the one remaining 10E although a fastener used to attach aluminum pieces does match the precisely drilled and spaced holes in said fragment.

Despite others who say it is a piece of a PBY or other aircraft, TIGHAR posits that this aluminum piece is a fragment torn from the fuselage by some force and claims that "TIGHAR Artifact # 2-2-V-1" is a large fragment of the patch that was installed in Miami which covered the rear, starboard window broken or cracked upon landing in Miami.

TIGHAR Director Gillespie theorizes that the patch was forcibly removed by Earhart and Noonan themselves in order to vent the hot aircraft after it landed on Gardner / Nikumaroro. That is possible and plausible.

Unfortunately, this is a highly controversial claim by TIGHAR due to the Alcoa company's practice of stamping or not yet stamping their *Alclad* aluminum with certain markings at that time. Critics of the TIGHAR claim point out that "ALCLAD" was not stamped on any aluminum used in aircraft until well after Earhart's flight and closer to the outbreak of WWII.

The aluminum fragment found by TIGHAR on the island does bear the faint marks "AD" (and another faint "D") which critics state absolutely precludes this piece as coming from Earhart's Electra. The counterclaim that this was a repair piece (not part of the original aircraft construction) and that aluminum sheeting for repairs were so marked has yet to be verified, to my knowledge, as no evidence of the use of the "ALCLAD" labeling at the time of Earhart's flight has been found so far.

Below is a diagram of Earhart's proposed eastbound flight route around the world but terminated at or before Howland Island.

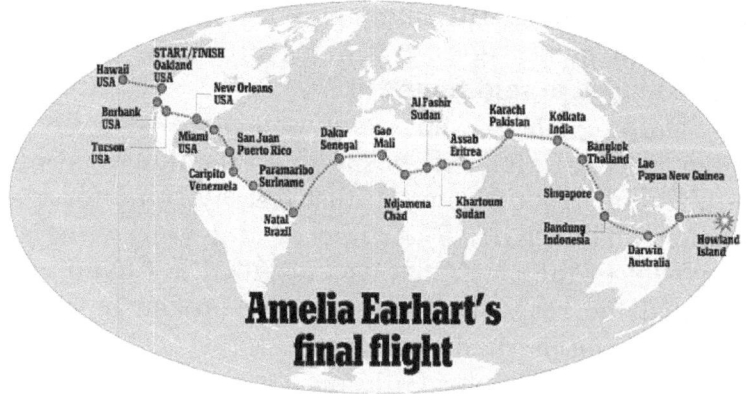

Amelia Earhart's final flight

Earhart and Noonan completed their flight or series of flight-legs eastbound up and until they landed at Lae, Papua, New Guinea. Here, they then prepared for the lengthy and most dangerous flight-leg to Howland Island, a distance of over 2,500 miles or 4,100 kilometers.

Howland Island is a mere 1.5 miles long by .5 miles wide or about 450 acres sitting just *20 feet* above sea level. Here, the Coast Guard ship *Itasca* waited for Earhart along with fuel, oil, and other provisions placed on Howland. The most important job for the ship's crew fell to the men in the radio room who were to guide Earhart and the Electra to a safe landing on one of the runways constructed on the island just for her flight.

Being very close friends with the First Lady, Eleanor Roosevelt, and the President certainly afforded Earhart ample opportunities for assistance. We might ask at this point, what President Roosevelt and possibly US Naval Intelligence expected in return for such a huge and expensive favor?

Online, I have seen an aerial photo of the Pacific Ocean dotted with cumulus clouds and their shadows, and the legend, *"Howland Island is in this photo."* The point is that the shadows cast by the clouds on a sunny day confuse the observer and hide the tiny island from pilot view.

The world circa 1937 had no radar (invented in 1935 but not in extensive use until 1939 in Britain), and no satellites or GPS. Navigational errors were common. I have already given you the eye-opening example of what happened to the *General Machado* flying from Cuba to Florida. Another notable and famous example of navigational error occurred during WW2 five years after Earhart's lost flight and fourteen years after the *General Machado* crashed.

In October 1942 famed WWI *ace* Eddie Rickenbacker was on board a B-17D and he was to tour American bases in the Pacific. Allegedly, he was also tasked with delivering a secret message of rebuke to General Douglas MacArthur from President Roosevelt for adverse remarks made by MacArthur about the President.

The navigator aboard the B-17D failed to find Canton Island (not too far from Nikumaroro in that region of the Pacific) and the plane was forced to ditch into the ocean. The survivors managed to stay alive for 24 days living on 3 days' rations, a seagull, rainwater, and fish they caught, or which jumped into their life raft, while they luckily went unnoticed by Japanese patrols before being found and picked up by Americans.

After he recovered, it is said that Rickenbacker did deliver the secret message to MacArthur. Amusingly, a newspaperman who had published an obituary story about Rickenbacker's life and untimely death in the Pacific issued a meme-like cartoon with the statement "Beg pardon, Eddie."

At the time Eddie Rickenbacker passed away, July 23, 1973, I was building a 1/6th scale, radio-controlled model of his Spad XIII from WWI. He was a hero and a great man.

The recent (Ballard) National Geographic special reported that the Electra's flight from South America to Africa saw a 150-mile navigation error by Noonan and Earhart and was a dangerous indication of what was to come in the flight over the vast Pacific Ocean to tiny Howland Island. I will assume that Earhart had radio communication at this point in her circumnavigation.

Radio direction-finding wasn't the only means by which Earhart and Noonan could make Howland by air. Celestial navigation, the responsibility of Fred Noonan, would also help them navigate.

A sextant is a device by which sightings on the Sun and the angle above the horizon can determine latitude or the distance above or below the Equator. Sextants also are made to "shoot the stars" for the same purpose when one is not on the surface of the ocean but at altitude. Clear skies are necessary for such precise observations and readings. Overnight clouds and haze during the Lae to Howland leg may have precluded Noonan from getting readings.

One Earhart fan who engaged me with his precise calculations of fuel consumption by the Electra which he claimed proved that Earhart could not have made it to Gardner or Nikumaroro, stated that the duo had good weather for their entire journey. How he divined 2400 miles of clear skies and no wind is from conditions at Lae and at *Itasca* or Howland. That is a far-fetched conclusion to extrapolate that to the entire 2400 mile air journey despite Earhart reporting early by radio about cumulus clouds and a *23 knot wind*.

Using a sextant and discerning latitude is only half of a "position" and could be anywhere on Earth on that line of latitude either above or below the Equator. Without knowing one's longitude or distance east or west of zero degrees or Greenwich, England, one cannot give or determine a definite or "accurate" position on the globe—*accuracy* is defined by the times and what navigators considered "close enough" at the time.

What is important in this calculation of longitude is a precise time-measuring instrument—a chronometer. If one's chronometer is set to the precise time at Greenwich, then one can determine one's longitude or distance therefrom. For centuries, the search for an accurate timepiece that would function aboard a sailing ship was the Holy Grail of navigation.

The British Government in the early 18th century offered a substantial prize of 20,000 British Pounds (a large fortune in those days) to the first person who could design a chronometer for shipboard use that would ensure accurate navigation within *thirty miles*.

John Harrison, a carpenter, took up the task and presented his first chronometer in 1735 with further development of additional, improved chronometers thereafter. He submitted for the prize and was ignored.

In 1763, the British Government decided to award him only 5,000 Pounds which they did not pay in full until another decade had passed. So much for gratitude!

Today, in London's Westminster Abbey, one can find Harrison's stone marker embedded in the floor, honoring him for his remarkable invention (see RGW 2018 photo below). Navigation enjoyed a renaissance of accuracy, and subsequent manufacturers improved on Harrison's device but kept his mechanism that allowed the clock to keep running while it was being wound, and therefore still accurate.

Also important to Earhart and Noonan were accurate weather reports. Headwinds meant heavy consumption of fuel and crosswinds meant being blown off-course over time; overcast conditions would mean that Noonan could not "shoot the stars" and accurately determine their position while in-flight. Adverse weather and visibility conditions at Howland Island would severely compromise a safe landing while the Electra was low on fuel and Earhart lacked sufficient time to search for the island.

According to W. C. Jameson in *Amelia Earhart, Beyond the Grave*, at Lae, one of the busiest airports in the world at the time, mechanics began a maintenance routine on the Electra. Engine parts were tested and replaced, internal parts of those repairs were ground to spec, and both engines achieved pressures within ¼ pound of each other. The oil in the engines was replaced and both engines ground-tested and air-tested in flight. The Electra was ready, and Earhart gave her approval.

At this point, July 1, the weather was not cooperating, and her departure was delayed. My fuel-calculating fan seemed to forget that local bad weather at Lae on July 1, 1937 had to travel *somewhere*. Why not along or across the very route she planned on taking? Additionally, radio problems cropped up. Earhart test-flew the Electra and then tried to take a fix on Lae's signal with her direction-finding equipment. This attempt failed. Earhart instead communicated by radio telephone with Lae. Earhart concluded that the reason for the failure was that Lae's signal was too strong and that she was flying too close to the airport.

This conclusion or decision by Earhart (which modern readers might think absurd) with no further testing, is counted and pointed to as an example of how foolhardy she was as she faced this dangerous and lengthy leg in her circumnavigation of the globe.

However, to be fair, this was a phenomenon known about radio at the time. There was thought to be a "dead zone" which might preclude someone close by from hearing a radio signal while another listener hundreds, even thousands of miles away could clearly hear said signal.

Radio use in aircraft was still in its infancy with less than a decade since radio had been adapted to aircraft use and the useful frequencies had been determined after much testing. Indeed, such was radio's primitive state that Earhart was advised to pitch her voice higher on a certain radio frequency so that she could be heard, intelligibly.

But the criticism is also fair. The pilots that I know all concur that they want a working radio before takeoff and that Earhart should have delayed until she found out what the problem was with her radio rather than assuming it was something to do with radio *phenomena*.

While they waited for the Electra to be serviced on Lae, Fred Noonan was upset because he was unable to hear or to receive the time signal broadcast from Australia that would permit him to precisely calibrate and align his chronometers. Remember that he needed an accurate time in order to calculate longitude. Radio stations daily broadcast a tone or time signal to keep world clocks accurate.

Although Noonan was known for his drinking, and Earhart's cryptic message in a cable (*personnel problems*) to her husband which implied that Fred Noonan was a problem, statements made after their disappearance said that Noonan didn't drink any alcohol or was not observed drinking while at Lae and only exhibited irritation about not getting his chronometers set properly—he had three. The accuracy of the chronometer and the time thereon was critical in calculating longitude and determining an accurate position especially for this long flight-leg to Howland Island.

Eventually, Lae officials asked for everyone in the area to maintain radio silence for a short period of time so that Noonan could receive the needed time-signal from Australia. This was accomplished successfully, and the three chronometers were duly calibrated. Imagine implementing such a radio broadcasting "timeout" today?

The Electra carried two types of gasoline. A 100-octane fuel in special tanks and used for takeoffs and 87-octane fuel for cruising. There was no 100-octane on Lae according to a mechanic's report still extant, but the report goes on to say that the Electra had plenty of the higher-octane "takeoff" fuel in her tanks from a refueling at a previous stopover.

Earhart had her Electra fueled to the maximum with 87-octane and, conscious of weight, proceeded to strip the aircraft of all non-essential items in order to save weight, achieve takeoff, and provide maximum fuel efficiency for the 2,500-mile flight. A planned departure on July 1 was postponed due to weather, and the pair took off in the Electra on the following day, July 2, 1937. This takeoff was captured on film and can still be viewed today. I also include the last known photo taken of Earhart and the man who supervised getting her airplane ready at Lae, New Guinea in the conclusion and last section of this work.

Observers wrote and spoke at the time that, during the takeoff, the Electra struggled to get into the air. It lifted off just before the cliff edge, dipped down toward the water, kicked up some spray with the propeller blast, and then rose into the sky. This description of the Electra's struggle for takeoff in warm air prompted many to speculate on what Earhart (while in flight) might have thought about Howland Island and its runways recently constructed for her use and that Howland was barely 20 feet above sea level. Landing there might be "easy" but taking off with a full load of fuel for Hawaii might see her plane crash into the ocean assuming the difference a cliff-edge and higher runway height above the water in Lae might mean compared to only 20 feet of airspace available at Howland Island with a runway that was not lengthy and in hot, thinner air.

The conclusion which Earhart may have drawn from the "dip" her aircraft took toward the water at Lae would mean crashing into the ocean at Howland with only twenty feet of altitude under her plane at takeoff there.

The added speculation about takeoff dangers must have also included the possibly warmer air temperatures at Howland which went to the plane's lift capability at takeoff, and which meant or forced her into considering carrying a lighter fuel load.

Fate intervened and the fliers never made it to Howland Island. But the speculation about that dangerous takeoff just 20 feet above sea level is valid. Also valid is the observation that Earhart and Noonan took off from Lae knowing that their direction-finding equipment had failed its flight test and had been unable to function properly.

This left only the radio and two frequencies she was using for her sole means of communicating and finding her way to tiny Howland Island. But her radio attempts failed at Lae. Let me interject at this point that one of these frequencies that Earhart relied upon (6210) was a frequency which *Itasca* had no voice broadcast capability though they might hear her broadcasting. They could transmit Morse on 6210 but neither Earhart nor Noonan were Morse-capable which left only the 3105 frequency for Earhart to hear *Itasca* broadcasts which she never did. My conclusion is that her radio receiver must have "burned out."

One might assume that for the shorter leg to Hawaii from Howland, Earhart would not have had a full fuel load on board for takeoff. The conclusion I reach is that Earhart knew she was flying to a veritable postage-stamp in the ocean and wanted as much fuel as possible to arrive in the vicinity such that if Noonan's dead-reckoning was off (possibly like it had been in Africa), she'd have enough fuel and therefore time to search for tiny Howland Island while presumably being guided in by radio fixes on her position, and vice-versa. Assumptions that were false, even foolish, in light of warning signs that all was not well with her radio equipment.

It is alleged that Earhart took off from Lae without receiving a weather report. I find that speculative and possibly misunderstood as to weather further along their intended route. Local conditions were certainly deemed good for takeoff. Sher was to pass over certain ships as she went eastbound. The takeoff of the Electra and subsequent reports about the takeoff provide the beginnings of controversy surrounding her flight, particularly the "trailing antenna" mentioned before. This antenna was installed below the fuselage and went aft toward the tail.

A ground crewman at Lae reported that parts of her antenna were found on the runway after she took off in the heavily fuel-laden Electra. It is alleged during takeoff that her aircraft or the antenna "kissed" the ground as she accelerated and was torn off. Was this ever communicated to her in-flight? Apparently not. However, there is a surviving film of that takeoff which was shown in the National Geographic special about the Ballard expedition. For an instant, a puff or cloud appears under the tail of the speeding and bouncing Electra to which many point to as the moment she lost the undercarriage's trailing antenna.

However, this puff or cloud may have been only the antenna's undercarriage brace (with no antenna wire attached) that touched the ground during the bumpy takeoff, or the wheels kicking up dirt that hit the wings and fuselage (more likely).

To the contrary, another source states that Earhart had that same antenna *removed* in Miami after the first leg of her flight. Regardless, either way, the Electra and Earhart did not have a piece of needed equipment necessary to hear signals in the 500 kilocycles radio frequency commonly used by naval vessels and used by *Itasca*.

Earhart used either of the two radio frequencies 3105 and 6210 depending upon the time of day. Apparently, Earhart was unaware that the *Itasca* could only listen on frequency 6210 because their radio had no voice transmission capability at this frequency nor could they find her position or direction using this frequency.

Also, neither Earhart nor Noonan knew Morse code sufficiently well to communicate in that code, a capability which the *Itasca had* on 6210 kilocycles— lacking only voice transmission capability. I will categorically state my belief here that had either Earhart or Noonan known Morse code, they would have made it—provided that they had a Morse key in the cockpit which it is reported they did not. Earhart had had it removed, supposedly.

These series of "fatal errors" compounded and contributed to her and her navigator's demise. I remind readers of the saga of the Pan Am flying boat *General Machado* and what looks to be an easy trip of just 90 miles and relatively easy navigation in 1928 from Cuba to Key West, Florida that resulted in a crash, fatality, and a 300-mile navigational error in just a few hours flying time because of unfactored winds in navigation.

What might ten hours of flying in <u>winds</u> of unknown speed and direction produce in navigational terms or errors therein? A mere 20 miles of wind speed perpendicular to their line of flight over ten hours might culminate in a navigational error of 200 miles north or south of their intended destination; headwinds or tailwinds of unknown force might put them well past their target or well short of it. Then, these problems did not take into account the radio problems that the fliers would face once they "arrived" in the vicinity of a half-square-mile target known as Howland Island with nothing but water and no landmarks to guide them, and a direction-finder they discovered still didn't work.

Here's what we do know. Shortly after takeoff, Lae radio heard Earhart report an altitude of 7,000 feet and a speed of 140 knots. Lae continued to relay weather reports to Earhart which were not acknowledged but may have been heard and the acknowledgements not heard since we don't know the true extent of the radio problems with Earhart's radio gear. She certainly could transmit!

An hour later, Earhart reported an altitude of 10,000 feet and a position of 150.7 degrees east (of Greenwich) and 7.3 degrees south (of the Equator) adding that she saw cumulus clouds. Two hours later, Earhart radioed a position of 4.33 degrees south Latitude and 159.7 degrees east Longitude, and that she was flying at an altitude of 8,000 feet over cumulus. Whether this was from a calculated position based upon fuel consumption and time flown, or a sextant or other navigational shot or sighting, or both, is not known. Earhart added that winds were at 23 knots.

Note that this latter position at 4.33 degrees south of the Equator corresponds with Gardner Island or Nikumaroro at 4.39 degrees south latitude. However, Nikumaroro is located at 174.32 west Longitude or across the international date line (approximately 26 degrees in longitudinal distance further into her flight). Earhart is flying northeast and approaching the Equator and dateline some four to five hours into her flight.

Why is that wind speed of 23 knots important? Over time, absent proper course correction, that 23 knot wind Earhart reported would affect the course they flew. In fact, simplistically, immediate course correction should be made such that the new course allows the wind to push the aircraft, over time, to its ultimate destination (that assumes a steady windspeed or vector affecting course).

Realistically, such course corrections were and must be ongoing as wind conditions vary throughout any air journey. We can only assume that Earhart's corrections for the wind acting on her aircraft were woefully inadequate such that she practically flew in a "straight" line or heading, arriving at the correct longitude for Howland Island but well south of her target in latitude.

The latter conclusion is my assumption because if she had arrived somewhere north of her target, she had Howland and another island to her south to find but saw nothing as she stated in her radio broadcast, "*We must be on you...but cannot see you....*"

On July 2, 1937, Earhart and Noonan were heading for the dateline and the unknown. That was her last, *heard* radioed position (4.33S by 159.7 E) placing her about 850 miles into her 2,500-mile leg and then on course for Howland Island. This means that for or during the next 1,650 miles of the Electra's flight, Earhart barely got above the Equator, and became lost due to a navigational error or a series of navigational errors— even lack of navigational information due to overcast, and a possible wind from the west or northwest that drove her airplane further south than she or Noonan realized.

Thereafter, the radio logs of *Itasca* record multiple transmissions to Earhart that were never acknowledged. At one point, Earhart promised to whistle into the microphone so that the waiting ship could take a bearing on her. They heard her whistle but were unable to contact her when she stopped whistling abruptly. The radiomen could not get a fix on her. Apparently, Earhart was unaware that she did not need to whistle and that she only needed to open her transmission for thirty seconds.

Then, apparently, Earhart did receive some signal from *Itasca*, but it was not of sufficient length or strength for her to obtain a bearing to *Itasca*. If true, then her radio reception problem was not total but intermittent—a possible sign of an antenna problem. Maddening to the *Itasca* radiomen, was that Earhart kept switching frequencies, and the men in the *Itasca* radio room "lost" her.

Earhart subsequently radioed that she was "200 miles out" (from Howland) and then "100 miles out" (guesses or estimates based upon perceived or calculated position from a last known "fix" or based upon flying time and fuel consumption and their heading). The *Itasca's* radiomen heard her whistling but not long enough for them to obtain a fix on her aircraft. It is safe to assume that Earhart did not know her true position which made Earhart any number of miles off course. There were reports that Earhart kept switching frequencies and didn't stay on a useable frequency long enough for the exasperated *Itasca* radiomen to get a fix. Earhart's radio competence as demonstrated by her entire Lae to Howland leg was practically nil which doomed her.

Even if they (Itasca radiomen) had heard her, and obtained a radio fix and bearing, <u>Earhart hadn't heard them,</u> and continued to broadcast that she could not hear the *Itasca* radio calls. So, even if they had a fix at that time, chances are they could not have communicated that to Earhart. However, such a fix might have made the subsequent search for the then missing duo more efficient.

Earhart's apparent lack of concern about radio communication is the biggest criticism leveled at her, and quite puzzling to experts and novices who have studied her flight. I will interject here that modern training for flight crews is very cognizant of cockpit arrogance, co-pilot deference to arrogant captains, and the fatalities caused by such. There is always the possibility that Earhart overruled Noonan's navigation and position readings as I will show, shortly.

Whether Earhart tried to use 500 kilocycles to communicate is unknown. The loss of or missing (removed) trailing antenna for use at 500 kilocycles and her lack of knowledge about 6210 kilocycles and the *Itasca's* incapability of voice or direction finding on that frequency meant that only 3105 kilocycles was useful in her circumstances for two-way <u>voice</u> communication. Trouble was, she did not know this. Did she suspect? Perhaps she did, but too late.

Frankly, it is difficult to accept that Earhart did not turn back to Lae, New Guinea when she apparently had no functioning two-way radio communication. Whether this is courage or foolishness (in those days) is still debated. Overconfidence can become foolhardiness especially flying over a vast stretch of the Pacific Ocean knowing that the duo had previous navigational errors of well over a hundred miles during this very circumnavigation attempt.

Close to her Howland Island destination, there followed radio messages from Earhart stating *"We must be on you but cannot see you."* The *Itasca* made smoke to assist Earhart in getting a visual. At one point a radioman heard her voice on the speaker come in so strongly that he rushed to the deck to try to spot the plane but was unable to locate it in the sky. This may have been attributable to the radio phenomenon previously described and *Itasca* was no longer in the "dead zone" and Earhart wasn't close at all but hundreds of miles off-course. And lost! She also might have been close and just over the horizon but confused enough to think she was north of Howland due to seeing nothing but open ocean and that she had to fly south to find Howland.

A word about vectors. Earhart reported wind speed of 23 knots according to the record of her broadcast of position. A line from Lae, New Guinea to Howland Island is a vector of direction including airspeed. Wind speed relative to her airplane is another vector of direction and speed that affects her course, and her groundspeed. Vectors are also calibrated such that their length equals a specific speed and the head of the arrow provides direction. For example, an air-speed of 150 mph, into a headwind of 50 mph, produces a ground speed of 100 mph.

Ironically, while Fred Noonan was serving aboard a Pan Am China Clipper in 1935 when Pan Am was gambling on starting their island-hopping Pacific service, the clipper turned about and returned to San Francisco due to vicious headwinds. A check of their fuel tanks in San Francisco after arrival revealed they had only a few minutes fuel left after flying 21 hours and 59 minutes in an aborted roundtrip in what should have been a 17 hour flight to Hawaii made impossible by headwinds (see https://www.panam.org/about/606-across-the-pacific-film).

Simply put, wind speed which Earhart reported was 23 knots, and that competing vector or wind's angle to the direction of flight, over time such as ten hours, could lead to being pushed off-course by as much as 230 nautical miles without course correction after the elapsed time of ten hours and her perceived arrival in the "vicinity" of Howland Island. Then, depending upon the direction of that wind, headwind or tailwind, a 23-mph wind might put Earhart 230 miles long or short of her destination, or somewhere between the two extremes. In the vast Pacific? There is no magical GPS or radar.

Radio communication and direction finding were lifelines. To fly without them working properly, fatal.

What course corrections were made in flight? What course corrections were possible from navigational instruments and weather conditions while in flight? We don't know. We do know that her last radio position put her 4.33 degrees south of the Equator with some 1,700 miles to go. We also know (will know from my photo discoveries) that she crash-landed on Nikumaroro at 4.39 degrees south of the Equator. Howland Island is at Zero degrees 48.5 *minutes* North or <u>above</u> the Equator. That is a huge error. Still, it's an error repeated by pilots through the years due to their negligence and inattention of whom Earhart is perhaps the most notorious.

It is speculated that weather and overcast conditions may have affected Noonan's ability to shoot the stars and get a positional fix. It is reasonable to conclude then that Earhart didn't fly 350 miles off-course to find Gardner or Nikumaroro after arriving in the area. What is more reasonable is to assume that, at arrival in what she believed to be the vicinity of Howland, she was somewhat off-course and, unsure of her position (mistaken position) and lost. Earhart flew north and south from being off course in the first place and didn't fly north far enough to spot and land on tiny Howland Island.

The navigation beacon she had installed on board the Electra was useless, the new device she had had uninstalled would have probably saved her since it allowed <u>simultaneous</u> voice communication (assuming her radio receiver was working).

Even assuming the wind vector's assumed perpendicular effect on her uncorrected course at 50% of the windspeed, that would place the Electra some one hundred and fifteen nautical miles *south* of Howland by the time she arrived in the area. This is pure speculation based upon the single wind speed she broadcast (that was *heard*) but certainly something to consider as to why she didn't arrive at Howland Island directly from Lae.

It is also possible that Fred Noonan caused or committed a whopping navigational error somewhere along the flight path like he had on their way to Africa in an earlier leg—off by *150 miles*. An overcast sky might have frustrated any navigational fix overnight. The weather was clear at Howland on July 2 but that didn't mean the weather was clear west or southwest of Howland while Earhart flew (she reported cumulus below her while flying at 8,000 feet but 1600 miles short of Howland).

At this point in the "vicinity" of Howland Island, it is estimated that Earhart had about four to five hours of fuel left. At her cruising speed of 140 knots that is 560 to 700 miles she could have or might have flown (altitude depending) in a desperate attempt to locate Howland Island or some other place to land. Earhart may have stretched that fuel somewhat more by leaning her mixture (adding more air to her fuel-mix).

Earhart was well-versed and experienced in landing her previous aircrafts *anywhere* when the plane or conditions required it. "Easy" enough to accomplish when you're over <u>land</u>.

More attempts at two-way communication were made but, inexplicably, according to the *Itasca* radiomen, Earhart did not keep talking on the same channel, nor did she keep her microphone open, and she kept switching frequencies. Nor did she continue to speak but instead made intermittent broadcasts. Being lost and searching the horizon is distracting, and distraction is the cause of many airplane crashes.

The fact that Earhart was unfamiliar with radio is glaringly obvious—and why wasn't Noonan on the radio thereby allowing Earhart to fly, undistracted? I doubt he was getting navigational fixes constantly. Earhart ruled in that cockpit.

It is possible that the aircraft radio was malfunctioning or unable to communicate with the waiting ship for some reason or due to radio phenomena peculiar to the technology at the time. It is also entirely possible that Earhart and Noonan were too focused on looking for Howland Island while keeping a wary eye on the fuel gauges. Then, it is quite possible that Earhart actually kept up a steady banter, but the ship's radiomen did not hear her except sporadically or because the signal was too weak, or because the parties were on different frequencies, or she had a broken tube. We don't know so we speculate.

Did Earhart utilize the old technology attached to the Bendix array? The aural-null indicator? Might she have been familiar with that from previous aircraft? It does give a bearing and a reciprocal for a radio signal detected. Might this be the origin of the "line" she said they were flying in her penultimate broadcast as "157/337?"

Just remember that logs were altered or sanitized per usual procedure afterward, and we only have a clean or sanitized log of what was <u>heard</u>. For all we know, Amelia Earhart broadcast a lot of unknown and unheard information.

In other words, we have only the *Itasca* radio log as to what was <u>heard</u> from Earhart as opposed to what might have been broadcast by Earhart but *not heard* aboard the waiting ship (for whatever reason or radio phenomenon).

Eventually, Earhart radioed that fuel was low and that she was running north and south on a line of 157/337 and that she would repeat this message on 6210 kilocycles.

"Wait..." was her last official word heard aboard *Itasca*. It was 8:43 or 8:44 a.m. local time and it was the last *in-flight* message heard from Earhart. Nevertheless, the ship's radiomen kept calling her and kept listening for any further radio signals. Perhaps she sighted something to her south which she thought was land or Howland and flew on.

The completed and sanitized or *clean* radio logs and the report submitted from the *Itasca* reveals that crew both on board and on Howland were somewhat put-out by Earhart's "stunt." A "clean log" is the official log made to make sense of the scribbles and crossed-out errors, etc. made during the actual broadcasts and log-recording.

The delays experienced by Earhart in Lae also meant delays for the readiness and reception committee of both *Itasca* and the shore party on Howland. After she was deemed lost and down, and after the largest air/sea rescue operation in history, newspapers published articles about banning such "stunts" in future. Itasca radiomen and naval personnel grumbled considerably because none of them wanted to be held to blame for Earhart's failure, disappearance, and death.

Apparently, the long hours in the radio room aboard *Itasca*, the exasperation with the many difficulties communicating in voice by radio with a duo that did not know Morse, and the radiomen's lack of success despite their best efforts, probably made for an edgy atmosphere aboard ship and in the radio room of *Itasca*.

One can understand the radiomen being fearful of being blamed should Earhart fail or perish. After she went missing, a natural tendency would then be to shift blame onto Earhart. Frankly, whoever advised Earhart about the Electra's radio and whoever was responsible for her communication abilities using said radio, miserably failed in their job of coordinating with the radiomen of *Itasca* prior to the fatal, final flight-leg.

Earhart had relied upon Paul Mantz for such things, apparently. A large part of any blame for her demise should be attributed to Mantz's failure to properly instruct Earhart in this regard. That is especially true of the 6210 frequency which only worked (voice) one-way—from Earhart to *Itasca*. Certainly, Mantz was or should have been aware of those limitations, or he failed to properly vet the matter with appropriate investigation and preparation.

Then, perhaps Mantz had too much faith in Fred Noonan as a navigator or Manning as a radio operator. He certainly should have reevaluated Earhart and this dangerous flight once Manning was off the team. Certainly, a few key questions and appropriate testing would have revealed such radio and communication limitations well beforehand. The conclusion, in fairness to Mantz, was that the radio in the Electra worked on the legs all the way to Lae.

What was the rush so late in the journey? A desire to get home? Boredom and fatigue must have played a significant role. And where was Fred Noonan in all this? He was a navigator and not a radioman. Noonan was the wrong man for the job? Another Earhart error? On the other hand, *whom* was an experienced navigator in that area of the world, the vast Pacific, at the time?

Fred Noonan with his experience with Pan Am and the Pacific Clippers and flying boats was a rare bird. Remember, they planned the trip to have three people on board which included Manning, an experienced radioman. Certainly, all their fuel calculations and weight allowances for the aircraft also included Manning's weight? So, why didn't Earhart get herself another radioman? That Earhart chose fuel for that saved weight of a missing navigator is the likely conclusion.

The answer to these allegations of folly may lie in the ground-loop accident in March 1937. All of Mantz's careful preparations for that <u>westbound</u> trip which included Manning were no longer in place when Earhart decided to try again and go <u>eastbound</u> around the world in late May of that year, without Mantz or Manning.

This begs the question; how could Amelia Earhart have been so cavalier about her plane's radio capabilities? Perhaps she had too great a faith in her ability as a pilot. The further question is why, near Howland Island, didn't Earhart continue to speak into her radio rather than broadcast sporadically as *Itasca* radio logs record? Or just hold the transmit key open for more than thirty seconds? Or give the microphone to Noonan and ask him to keep up a banter? Maybe she did speak, or held the frequency open, but she wasn't heard at the time though heard in other instances.

Part of that answer might lie with what I stated earlier about the direction-finding equipment both new (removed and replaced) and old. The older system did not permit simultaneous broadcasting and direction finding. With the old system reinstalled, Earhart had to speak and then listen for a response and not transmit—a delay that proved costly (she also had to fly the plane). Perhaps, not hearing any response, a sense of panic contributed to Earhart's constant changing of frequencies.

A pilot flies the plane, and Noonan (was he always in the rear of the Electra?) should have been on the radio and looking for Howland, or assisting in some way beyond navigational calculations that, in hindsight, we know had to be wrong or possibly ignored, perhaps impossible to take due to overcast local to the aircraft until he took a sun shot at dawn on (the repeated day due to dateline crossing) July 2, 1937.

Was Noonan correct with the navigational information given Earhart that morning? If so, then did Earhart overrule Noonan? All that empty ocean flying North erroneously convincing her to fly south to Howland? The strong radio signal and her loud voice heard aboard Itasca is a clue that what was just described is exactly what happened when Earhart had the misfortune to turn south too soon.

Had Earhart retained the new navigation and direction-finding equipment her fate might have probably been different. Remember, an experienced pilot on the *General Machado* turned left into the Gulf of Mexico while believing he was further east of Florida and was unaware of the crosswind that had carried that flying boat well to the west of the state. Two years later in the vast Pacific? I have no trouble seeing the scenario of the *General Machado* being replayed by Earhart and Noonan aboard the Electra.

Confirmation bias can be deadly: *There's nothing but open ocean between Howland and China. I'm seeing nothing but open ocean and cannot see or hear Itasca...therefore, Fred Noonan must be wrong and I must be north of Howland and must fly south to find it and Itasca.*

Such is fate and how small, even tiny mistakes, can cascade and add up to disaster. The *Titanic* scenario is the quintessential example of such and comprises a lengthy list full of "If only..." which, if only "it" had occurred or not occurred, the chain of cascading disasters would have been broken, and *Titanic* would not have foundered.

We know that Earhart couldn't hear the *Itasca* (except once, faintly) which means we must cast blame on her radio equipment, a possible faulty antenna, her lack of knowledge about the equipment, her apparent lack of use of said equipment, and her fateful decision to remove the new direction-finding gear and replace it with an older, thought more reliable, set of gear. Then, we must return to the ground loop incident on Oahu in her first attempt and the subsequent loss of a competent radioman (Manning) who quit the team out of fear of Earhart's competency as a flier.

Note that in the past, with the exception of flying to the Hawaiian Islands from Oakland, Amelia Earhart always flew toward large masses of land which makes finding places (or alternate landing areas) a lot easier than finding less than a square mile of atoll in the middle of the Pacific. Then, Hawaii has multiple islands which are relatively large. The very size of Africa and the landmass before her "saved" her on the South America to Africa leg of her round the world flight despite a huge navigational error of some 150 miles as reported in the October 2019 "Expedition Amelia" broadcast.

Surely, her memories of her first transatlantic flight as a passenger which made her famous should have also reminded her of the large navigational error committed on *that* flight. But it did not, apparently. Her husband, Putnam, told her to cancel the trip when he cabled her in Lae, and he asked her to come home.

Had she not crashed her plane during takeoff in March 1937, I believe success for her original westbound attempt at circumnavigation at the Equator was practically assured though she still would have had to fly from Hawaii to some point or atoll for refueling such as Howland Island. Certainly, that was in place when she attempted takeoff and unfortunately, ground looped.

Note that Earhart also might have struck a deal with Pan Am and used Midway, Wake, and Guam as legs and refueling stops which only somewhat compromised her *closest to the Equator circumnavigation of the globe* by a meaningless number of miles.

Pan Am had built runways and radio towers on these islands (two were uninhabited). Earhart didn't need to use *Itasca* or FDR's help. Cost? I'm sure Pan Am would have charged her a lot of money to use their facilities despite the promotional possibilities.

Returning to my speculation about her first westbound attempt, Earhart would have had a radioman on board whose experience (and knowledge of Morse Code) would have probably seen her find Howland Island, handily, on what would have been her second flight leg, the longest and most dangerous over the open Pacific.

My conclusion is that a fatigued Earhart was confused as she approached Howland Island or its vicinity that fateful morning. For whatever reason, possibly Noonan's navigational error, or lack of a fix, or mistake, I speculate that Earhart thought she was north of Howland when her flight time and fuel consumption told her she was close or a hundred miles out. Much like the errors made by even modern aircraft due to pilot confusion such as US Navy *Flight 19* or Varig *Flight 254*, Earhart knew that north of Howland there was only China which was thousands of miles away. After seeing nothing but open ocean and no land, she flew south expecting to come upon Howland from the north.

Speculating further, it is quite possible that the moment when the radioman went out on deck after hearing her strong signal, Earhart may have been just fifty miles away but then turned south thinking she was north of Howland. That is confirmation bias (seeing empty ocean) at its worst and proved momentarily safe when Nikumaroro came into view but proved to be ultimately deadly.

Did Earhart overrule Noonan? Is this why Noonan was and sounded so angry and bitter in what are known as Betty Klenck's notes which a fifteen-year-old in Florida wrote down as she listened on a Fourth of July weekend, probably on late Friday afternoon, July 2, on her father's shortwave radio shortly after Earhart and Noonan crash-landed? Earhart cut through Noonan's pain, anguish, calling out to his wife, and his fear of the tidal water coming into the plane with, *Will you help me?*

Betty's notes are a fascinating peek at that historic moment, and we'll take a good look at them later in this book.

Again, such is fate, and such is the endless speculation and "What if...?" which goes on to this day.

3

The Search for the Missing Flyers

We are flying on the line 157/337....

The line of 157/337 which Earhart referred to in her radio message is not a line of "position" but represents Earhart's radioed headings as she flew back and forth over the ocean desperately looking for Howland Island as her fuel ran low. Unfortunately, no one, not even Earhart or Noonan, knew her actual position. As stated earlier, possibly Noonan knew their actual position but Earhart overruled him.

Earhart was lost, and most likely confused due to believing she was north of Howland (why else did she fly south all the way to Nikumaroro or Gardner Island?). Somehow, the navigation was off. Allegedly, Earhart carried no chart for the area south of the Equator which helps explain why, just assuming for the moment that she landed on Nikumaroro or Gardner Island, Earhart did not know the name of the island and why she never mentioned the name in her post-crash broadcasts heard by many.

What a difference that would have made had post-crash radio listeners heard her repeated call, mentioning not a "reef" or "little island" but *"Gardner Island."* Even if she had known the name of the island, the one she crash-landed on *did not resemble* the shape of the island presented on charts at the time as being Gardner. That was only corrected to all new maps and charts in 1938 and entirely due to the new intelligence the search and rescue added to our knowledge of the Pacific Ocean in that area. Additionally, Howland was mis-charted by five nautical miles at the time. Can you imagine

Earhart's confusion when she spotted Gardner (Nikumaroro) which resembled nothing close to Howland?

Another example of fate and tiny mistakes adding up to total disaster.

We can also assume at the time she broadcast her "line" that Earhart either neglected to say her flying direction or the radio failed to transmit her entire message and what direction she was flying at the time on that "line" of 157/337.

In fairness, consideration must be given to the fact that we have only the *Itasca* radiomen's logs as to what they *heard* on the frequencies they were listening to. This does not mean that Amelia Earhart was not transmitting. It is possible that Earhart did broadcast a lot of chatter that was simply unheard aboard *Itasca* owing to being on the wrong frequency, equipment anomalies, or known radio phenomena that prevented reception.

I can't speak for how many radio receivers around the world were listening in at this important climax to the Lae to Howland leg while she searched for Howland Island. Certainly, after Earhart was reported down, great numbers of radio receivers around the world tuned in to 3105 and 6210. Many reported hearing her voice on the shortwave frequencies she used including hearing her say her call sign.

Among these people listening were many Japanese radio enthusiasts who reported to their government that they believed the "post-crash" signals they heard came from the *Phoenix Islands* – Kiribati! This tidbit of information is in the final search report filed by the captain of the US Navy's carrier *Lexington* and easily read on the US National Archive website.

These reports or "post-crash radio signals" are helpful to us in our analysis of her disappearance and of her crash-landing on Nikumaroro or Gardner.

Flying such compass bearings, 157/337, 180 degrees apart, could be performed anywhere on Earth including from the very seat you are in while reading this book. What is needed is a fixed point from or to which one of those headings is being made such that a line drawn on a chart can be viewed with some accuracy to see where it either intersects or comes close to some convenient or likely, alternate landing spot.

For your own participation in our armchair rescue endeavor, use Google Earth and, using "tools," draw a navigation line between Howland Island and Nikumaroro. North-Northwest of Howland is empty ocean all the way to the Asian mainland on heading 337 but south of Howland on heading 157 that *line* passes within 2.5 degrees of Nikumaroro. Did no one plot that line using Howland Island as a base? Apparently not or at least not until *Itasca* changed course and began to head south per the newspaper article and transcript I will describe in a later chapter.

Perhaps, another instance of "fate?"

Eventually, time passed after her last radio message with nothing further heard from her by the radiomen of *Itasca*. If she had continued flying for this time period, it was reasoned, then Earhart must have run out of fuel and was down, somewhere. The *Itasca* captain guessed it was somewhere <u>north</u> of Howland. Fair to say that Earhart also assumed she was north of Howland while seeing only empty ocean. The same mistake and why? Was the captain aware of wind from the south or southeast, locally? We don't know.

Meanwhile the *Itasca* began to search north and east and west of Howland Island for any sign of the downed flyers based upon the assumption that she had gone down north of the intended destination of Howland Island.

Then, assistance was summoned and the greatest ocean search for downed flyers began which eventually included the carrier *Lexington*, the battleship *Colorado*, dozens of other military ships, and many aircraft— including resources provided by the *Japanese Empire.*

Among these ships searching for Amelia Earhart and the Electra was the Imperial Japanese Navy (IJN) Ship *Koshu*. Do remember that name! Also, it was reported in newspapers in Japan and then picked up by western press that a "Japanese fishing boat had picked up the flyers." The latter report was hastily withdrawn and retracted a few days later. This is also important because whenever I mention "some other Japanese ship" (picking up the two flyers) I am implying this very fishing boat as the only plausible way to get both flyers from Nikumaroro and into the hands of the Japanese before July 9, 1937 when the USS Colorado seaplanes flew over and around Nikumaroro.

The aerial photos of the Electra airplane wreckage are from Nikumaroro and from photos of the shipwrecked SS Norwich City 1938-1942 (as presented to you earlier) but not taken by the USS Colorado seaplanes on July 9, 1937 (they took one known photo of Gardner which reveals little at the altitude it was taken.

Additional ships sailed from Hawaii and the west coast of the USA for Howland Island, and this took time. Upon arrival at Howland, the USS *Colorado* used her catapults to launch seaplanes to search the ocean and nearby islands for any sign of the missing flyers and the Electra.

On July 9, 1937, a week after Earhart's disappearance on July 2, these seaplanes from *Colorado* flew around and surveyed Gardner Island but only sighted the shipwrecked *Norwich City* and neither plane wreckage nor survivors waving from the beach were to be seen.

The report of Lambrecht who was in command of these three flying planes from the battleship *Colorado* is revealing for several reasons: *one,* the charts and positions of certain "reefs" and "atolls" to the south of the *Colorado* were incorrect or non-existent which prompted Lambrecht to poke fun at those sailors who swore they spotted a reef in such and such a position where he and his companion-seaplanes turned up nothing but empty ocean; and *two,* is his report that, at each island, they saw no sign of the aircraft or the missing duo despite flying around these atolls at a thousand feet and "zooming" or buzzing the area at a lower altitude, repeatedly.

Lambrecht and the *Colorado's* seaplanes found "nothing," but the report does have some intriguing detail worth discussing (see later in this narrative); the *third* or number three reason is that all maps or charts pre-1938 had the wrong shape of Gardner Island (Nikumaroro), and this was not corrected on charts and maps until the year following Earhart's disappearance. And reason number *four* which is of great interest, is that the seaplane crews saw "*signs of recent human habitation*" on Gardner Island. This might possibly have been the shelter constructed by the shipwrecked sailors of the *SS Norwich City* in 1929 or extant structures from the abandoned nineteenth century coconut plantation and operation.

It is possible that Earhart knew the shape of Gardner Island from a remembered chart but the shape of the island below her flying aircraft did not match and must have further confused her when it did not match any islands *north* of the Equator or near Howland (on charts she must have had). The shipwreck itself was also a surprise to the pilots and observers in the *Colorado* seaplanes, and no doubt also to Earhart and Noonan, because none of them knew of such a shipwreck. Though, the hopeful duo must have thought they were close to shipping lanes.

If Earhart landed there on Gardner Island, it is no wonder she had no idea where she was. I've seen allegations in my online readings that Earhart carried no charts for this part of the Pacific that was below the Equator. Hence, no listener of post-crash radio signals ever heard the name "Gardner Island" mentioned by Earhart. But note that Betty Klenck, listening on her father's shortwave radio and making notes at the time did state that Earhart kept saying "New York City" or "something like that." Which Betty abbreviated as NYC in her notebook. Earhart kept repeating the only man-made landmark she could identify—the shipwreck *Norwich City*.

Earhart could not say what she did not know. Whether this was from complete ignorance or from confusion due to the shape of the island on her out-of-date chart, depended upon whether she had such a chart with her or she remembered seeing Gardner on some other chart prior to her flight.

Note also the <u>charted</u> false reefs and shoals that the *Colorado's* seaplanes failed to find and which Lambrecht or the Captain of the *USS Colorado* poked fun at in the written report of their search made by said Captain. Earhart wasn't the only one with out-of-date charts or charts containing erroneous information. Lambrecht and his flying team were also completely surprised to see the shipwrecked *Norwich City* on Gardner Island because they had no prior knowledge that the wreck was there.

Per the *Colorado* captain's report, at Gardner Island, the pilots and observers aboard the seaplanes reported that they saw "signs of recent human habitation." This intriguing remark in their report is not elaborated upon. In fact, no one had set foot on Gardner Island since the 1880's (except a science team in the early 1920s, and the shipwrecked crew of the *Norwich City* in November 1929).

One wonders exactly what "signs of habitation" the pilots and their observers observed on Gardner and where. Was it the shelter made by the *Norwich City* crewmen opposite the bow of their stranded ship? Those five words about recent habitation were not enough for the captain of the USS Colorado to request a ground search of Gardner Island, apparently. Such thinking is disturbing. I can only assume that Lambrecht clarified that in some oral remarks made to his commanding officer or to the captain, himself. Then, a week without fresh water on an island with no fresh water source may have seen Earhart and Noonan dead or near dead with delirium on July 9 when the Colorado seaplanes flew overhead. Earhart is alleged to have been overheard broadcasting "...*can't last much longer*..." on July 7, 1937.

One of the pilots did manage to snap a photo of Gardner Island which reveals nothing except a high or approximately 750 feet altitude shot of a presumably empty beach at the southern tip of the island (the shipwreck is on the northern tip). No other photos have been found or mentioned in reports from that time.

A TIGHAR helicopter video of Nikumaroro available on their website reveals how people on the island (TIGHAR members) are not visible at a thousand feet or even visible from a few hundred feet in altitude. With an erroneous north arrow (it points west), here is the only known photo taken by the Colorado's seaplanes at approximately 1,000 feet in altitude from the southeastern tip of Gardner (possibly on next page).

Not much to see, is there? Amazing to think that this is the *only time* that a visitor to Nikumaroro didn't photograph the shipwreck! It's on the opposite side of the island in the above photograph. I'm sure they did take a photo, but the photo is lost or yet to be located.

At Gardner Island, there was the *Norwich City* which ran aground in a storm and heavy seas in November 1929 that lead to a fire, an evacuation in the heavy seas and surf, with the loss of 11 crew drowned out of 35. According to the report and inquiry into the grounding, the three washed-up and recovered bodies were buried in the beach area opposite the bow of the grounded wreck.

Over the years, heavy seas and surf probably washed these bodies out to sea (possibly even inland and into the lagoon) or exposed them to crabs, or crabs exposed the remains and did the rest of the disinterring.

Anecdotal (spoken) evidence provided by a woman (a young girl at the time), whose father was a carpenter on Nikumaroro, is that her father made a wooden box to house the many bones found in the vicinity of the shipwreck which were then transferred to Suva, Fiji. Was this independent of the later bones found in 1940 on the southern shore which (governor or magistrate) Gallagher attributed to Earhart, and which were also transferred to Fiji, or at the same time?

This Gilbert Islander lived there on Nikumaroro during 1938-1941, and interviewed six decades later, spoke of bones, many bones near the "plane" and how her father, a carpenter, had made a box for the bones for "Mr. Gallagher" who would write a top-secret report that these bones may have been the remains of Earhart (Earhardt *sic* in report). These very bones in that box that went to Suva, Fiji are still searched for to this day, and thought to be on the island of Tarawa.

Some critics accuse this former inhabitant of being "coached" to include statements about an airplane and airplane parts. A fatuous accusation at best because even Ric Gillespie's bit of aluminum claimed to be a bathroom window patch and found there on Nikumaroro bears many marks of a blade or kitchen implement because the aluminum piece was used as a cooking surface.

Then, there is the unpleasant possibility that the thousands of giant coconut crabs (lengths of up to 3 feet) that inhabit the island which disinterred the seamen's bodies for food consumption, littering the reef near the *Norwich City* wreck with bones, also fed on and devoured the corpses of Amelia Earhart and Fred Noonan.

Luckily, the crew of the *Norwich City* had managed to send a distress or *mayday* call and position before evacuation and, within a few days, were taken off the island with great difficulty. There was no landing area at the atoll and the dangerous reef had to be traversed going in and coming out with extreme difficulty even for the seasoned and experienced islanders from other islands in the Gilbert and Ellice chain who participated in that rescue.

Eventually, decades later, a section of the reef was blown up with explosives to form a channel through the reef to facilitate landing small boats for the abandonment of the island in 1963 and is still used to this day though highly dangerous and unpredictable in heavy surf and high tides.

Yes, it is entirely possible that the "signs of recent habitation" on Gardner Island seen by the searchers in the *Colorado's* seaplanes may have come from sighting the temporary shelters and ship's stores the crew of the shipwrecked *Norwich City* took onto the island (or remnants of the 1880's habitation) and which were still visible from the air some eight years after the shipwreck (1929-1937) or over fifty years after the failed coconut plantation (1885-1937).

However, the record is silent as to exactly what gave the *Colorado* airmen this impression at Gardner Island although Lambrecht's report does report zooming to lower altitudes over abandoned structures on <u>another</u> abandoned or uninhabited island. It is easy to see how minds too easily eliminated Gardner Island as a possible landing site for Earhart and Noonan.

Furthermore, if these flyers were over Gardner island at high tide, the submerged Electra (now with both landing gear broken) would not have been visible unless they flew directly over it and were looking down into the water. Especially not visible considering the surprise distraction afforded by the imposing bulk of the shipwreck itself, and the fact that no one until me, as far as I know, has ever spotted the Electra *hidden* amongst the rusty debris in those aerial photos.

On July 18th, the search was called off by the U.S. Government. Amelia Earhart and Fred Noonan were deemed officially lost at sea, "officially dead." But were they dead on July 18, 1937? In fairness to the capture theory advocates, I believe they were *possibly alive* but not well-off. I also consider the possibilities that they were near death, or dead on the island.

I believe fate might have had a different ending in store for the duo if we believe the evidence presented by proponents of the Japanese capture Earhart theory.

The photo below (possibly on next page) is of *Itasca*. The ship that waited for Earhart at Howland Island and which tried but failed to communicate with her during her flight.

US Coast Guard, *Itasca*.

4

Strange Radio Signals

Amelia Earhart's popularity and her reported disappearance during her attempt to circumnavigate the globe caught the public's attention and that of the press. It was a media frenzy on or after July 2, 1937 as hopes soared on every piece of news, real or not, about Earhart's and Noonan's fate.

America loved and adored Amelia Earhart.

Yes, the press, Coast Guard, and authorities received numerous reports from amateur ham radio operators that they had heard Earhart's call sign on the frequency she broadcast on long after she supposedly went down. Some of these were outright hoaxes. Some reports about signals from Earhart were actually listeners misled by the radio play on a show called *March of Time* which they happened to catch on the airwaves. This radio play was a dramatic recreation of Earhart's final message and a made-up story of the aftermath purely for entertainment purposes. However, the recreation was first broadcast on July 8 and postdates most reliable reports of post-crash signals on Earhart's frequencies.

Hoaxes didn't help the truth and perhaps contributed to the general dismissal of reports of post-crash radio signals allegedly heard from Earhart as hoaxes or fantasy by authorities and searchers for Earhart who did bitterly complain in their reports that it didn't help matters.

However, there were plenty of credible sources as well. Robert Ballard admitted in the National Geographic TV broadcast *Destination Amelia* that he could not ignore that radio evidence and direction-finding from numerous radio sources at the time of her disappearance which radio signal bearings on the mystery signals heard on 3105 and 6210 pointed to and intersected at Nikumaroro, formerly known as Gardner Island.

Other official and more credible sources included military radio operators in Hawaii and other islands who reported hearing a series of dashes on that frequency (three for "on land" and four for "on sea" which had been agreed upon with Earhart), and those reports stated these radio signals were triple dashes (consistently sticking to an "on land" message). Remember, Earhart and Noonan had very limited Morse code capability—a single, repeated letter at best.

Officials and searchers were made aware that for Earhart's radio to be working, the plane had to be above water (on land) so that the engine could be run. Some radio listeners were able to take a bearing on said post-crash signals. Pan American Airways had a radio and direction finder on Mokapu Point on Oahu (and other stations in the Pacific) which serviced their Pan Am Clipper fleet. They also got a bearing but reported and labeled it as "doubtful...."

This bearing was <u>213 degrees</u>. I'll say it here, this is not doubtful at all. Run a line on google Earth from Mokapu Point, Oahu with a bearing or heading of 213 degrees. What island do you come near? No surprise but it's Gardner or Nikumaroro island.

If you don't understand what a navigational *bearing* is, imagine you are surrounded by a circular protractor of 360 degrees, a bearing is any line from your body to a degree marking on the circumference of the protractor—a bearing or direction from a fixed spot. Likewise, it constitutes a bearing from a <u>specific place or position</u> on a map or chart.

If one takes the various bearings from these reliable radio stations and direction-finders in July 1937 and plots them on a map, they all intersect near Gardner Island now known as Nikumaroro as was demonstrated by Ric Gillespie of TIGHAR during the "Destination Amelia" television broadcast. Robert Ballard found this radio "multiple-bearings" evidence to be very significant and impossible to ignore. Gillespie isn't the originator of this evidence nor the so-called "Nikumaroro Hypothesis" of where Amelia Earhart crash landed. Fred Hooven is responsible, and his meticulous research began the idea that Earhart had landed on Gardner or Nikumaroro.

Naturally, we are viewing matters in hindsight and most people today are not overly cognizant of the limitations of radio technology in 1937 or radio technology in aircraft. Nor are most people generally aware of the limitations of ships and planes at that time as far as speed, fuel, and range are concerned, especially in the vast Pacific. Many are unaware of the shocking lack of accuracy of charts in this region of the Pacific. It is only in 1935 that Pan Am gambled on making a flying boat a flying gas tank just to prove they could fly to Hawaii. Passenger service on Pan Am "Clippers" had only just commenced at the time Earhart disappeared.

This intersecting point (grouping) of multiple direction finders for the radio signals purported to be from Earhart was 350 miles south of Howland Island and defied belief as to how it was possible for Earhart to be so far off course. I've explained this before about how a small wind over an extensive flying time can lead to being off course by hundreds of miles. I can't answer for why people were not accepting of this fact then or even today unless they have an overstated estimate of Amelia Earhart's or Noonan's navigational skills.

Even Eddie Rickenbacker's pilot and navigator in WWII erroneously navigated to a Pacific ocean crash landing, missing the intended island destination completely. My discoveries of the plane wreckage in those vintage aerial photos clinches Earhart's place of crash landing as Nikumaroro or Gardner just like Fred Hooven correctly predicted decades ago. Yes, Fred Hooven did waffle and disavow his theory but only because he couldn't prove it and he was assailed by the so-called "experts" who shouted him down. Ric Gillespie and TIGHAR then took up the theory as their own quest for finding Earhart's aircraft.

In Earhart's case, an additional ten hours flying from her last heard radio position broadcast would equal up to 230 miles off-course from her target destination if the 23-knot wind she reported was perpendicular to her line of flight and endured. Did wind velocity increase? Did she fail to correct? Or correct enough? Unknown, except she was off course by hundreds of miles if you believe I've shown you her aircraft wreckage on the reef next to the *Norwich City*'s stern, then her bow six months later, and a shot from the port side where the aircraft is a hundred meters or so from the point where it will pass the shipwreck, port to starboard. Surely, the June 1941 photo is enough of a miracle shot of a Lockheed Electra in what has to be the most perfect and serendipitous timing between two waves, ever?

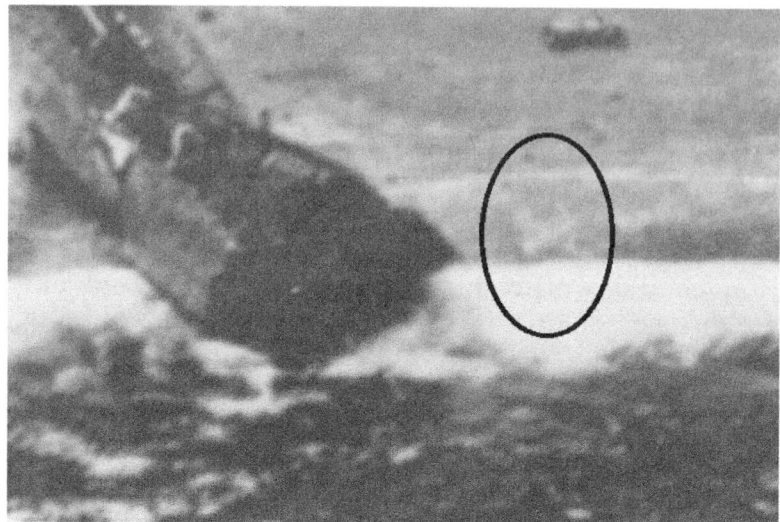

At those radio frequencies that Earhart used, it was known that a radio signal could bounce off the atmosphere and be heard thousands of miles away. Pan Am used it to radio their island landing stations. And those post Earhart crash signals *were heard* in New England, Saint Petersburg, Florida, Vancouver, and New Brunswick, Canada, and even Wyoming (Japan, too). The problem was sorting what was real news and persons actually hearing Earhart broadcasting as opposed to what was either a hoax or an overheard radio play.

There were hoax broadcasts. But let's visit what are deemed more reliable listeners including the military and civilian professionals who caught the transmission of "dashes" on that frequency (Earhart and Noonan knew a little Morse Code, enough to signal a repeated three dash transmission or single letter.

Betty Klenck, age fifteen, listening to her father's shortwave radio boosted by an extended outdoor antenna he had installed in the backyard of their Saint Petersburg, Florida home, heard Amelia Earhart's voice and listened. While doodling in her notebook, Miss

Klenck wrote down the fragments of the sentences she heard spoken by both Earhart and Noonan including lists of numbers which, to her young mind, might be some sort of position and therefore important.

We do not know on what date Betty Klenck heard these signals, whether July 2 or thereafter, nor could she recall the date when interviewed before her death. From her still extant "notes" made at the time, I believe a reasonable inference is that Betty Klenck heard Earhart and Noonan right after they landed on July 2. I believe my conclusion to be a reasonable inference for the following reasons. There is much talk between Earhart and Noonan of rising water, Noonan being hurt, and Earhart pleading with Noonan to help her. Once he had evacuated, I doubt a panicked and injured Noonan ever got back into that airplane on the edge of the reef!

However, Betty Klenck didn't merely listen. She and her father dutifully reported what she had heard to the local Coast Guard only to be brushed off, apparently by a remark to the effect that "We've got ships in the area" or something similar. Betty Klenck kept that notebook all her life and "Betty's Notes" (original copies) are easy to find online (TIGHAR website) and make for fascinating reading.

There on just a few pages in that precious notebook, the words of both Earhart and Noonan are written down as best Betty <u>heard</u> and understood them. Several times, Betty wrote down "NY" or "something like that" which she said in an interview was her abbreviation for what sounded to her like "*New York City.*"

For the proponents of the scenario that Amelia Earhart landed on Nikumaroro or Gardner Island, the references to "NY" or the full city name (New York City) sounds very similar to the name of the 1929 shipwreck there on the reef, the *Norwich City*. Listening on a shortwave radio to a carrier signal fading in and out, it is easy to understand the similarity of sound. For Earhart, obviously not knowing the name of the island, the hulking wreck with the name still visible on the hull must have filled her with hope as a landmark pinpointing where she had landed, and possibly known to those searching for her because it was near shipping lanes.

Unfortunately, even Lambrecht who was in charge of the three seaplanes from the *Colorado* was amazed and surprised to see a shipwreck on the reef at Gardner Island. Apparently, neither he nor the other five crewmembers knew of the wreck. It had been forgotten. It would appear that, other than the British Admiralty and Lloyds of London, no others involved in the search were aware of this shipwreck. Assuming any of the active searchers misheard either Earhart and Noonan say "New York City" as Betty Klenck did, they would be just as clueless about the reference and the like-sounding name *Norwich City* (usually mispronounced by anyone not British as *Nor-wich* instead of *Norrich*).

To my knowledge, no one other than Betty Klenck heard "NYC" (New York City) or what sounded like that. Then, possibly no one else kept a notebook for seven decades of what they had heard Earhart and Noonan say in which Betty had written down their words at the time or what she considered to be important. A dramatic, radio recreation of Earhart's last minutes of flight was performed on July 8 on the radio broadcast *March of Time*. Betty Klenck was not listening to that drama. How do I know? Not one of Betty's notes and written, overheard words originates from the script of that radio play.

We, on the other hand, are very much influenced by hindsight. However, in our armchair search for Earhart, we will use and rely upon this reference and "fact" and the teenager's precious notebook. By inference, I make those notes as being written on July 2, 1937 right after Earhart landed and cracked-up on Nikumaroro or Gardner Island reef at approximately 10:00 local time and about 1600 to 1630 hours EDT at Betty Klenck's home. Yes, that area of the Pacific was in a time zone that was an additional half-hour behind Hawaiian time.

It was a Friday, the beginning of the 4th of July weekend. Betty jotted down a time on the second page; Noonan was there in the cockpit; the water was rising; panic was evident in Noonan's voice; Earhart asked for help. Noonan, apparently injured, cries out to his wife, calling her by name *Marie-Oh!* (Mary Bea actually, but Klenck heard it phonetically as *Marie*). Noonan is not heard from again. I doubt Noonan had the courage or good health enough to wade out to the plane on the reef to help Amelia work the radio when low tide allowed propeller clearance.

A reef landing is possible at Gardner / Nikumaroro at low tide and the nearby shipwreck may have given the fliers hope that they were near shipping lanes. The reef is "always wet" except at unusually low tides and the average water depth (a meter) depends upon the tides.

Betty's notes reveal that the voices of Earhart and Noonan which she heard on her father's shortwave radio were concerned about rising water which gives proponents of this scenario further evidence of their hypothesis since Earhart would have had to run the engine with the propeller clear of the rising water in order to broadcast and charge the battery that powered the radio. In fact, all broadcast times of these credible post-crash radio signals occurred at low tide on Gardner / Nikumaroro. Robert Ballard mentioned this in the recently broadcast National Geographic special, *Destination Amelia*—a fact that Ballard noted as very significant in addition to noting the consistency of the radio bearings all intersecting near Nikumaroro.

Add to this that landing wheel in the "Bevington photo" from 1937 taken by Cadet Bevington, which possibly indicates that Earhart could not maneuver her aircraft because a landing gear collapsed while landing much as they did on Oahu when she ground looped. Her aircraft was subject to the tides as was the important engine for powering the radio. Note that the report filed by the Captain of the *USS Lexington* mentioned that a radio broadcast had been heard allegedly from Earhart that they were on a little island reef with a broken wing about 200 miles (closer to 350 miles) south of Howland Island. Further note that Japanese listeners and direction finders reported at the time that these radio signals came from the Phoenix Islands or Kiribati – Nikumaroro or Gardner Island being one of eight atolls in the chain.

Then, from these notes of Betty Klenck's and other listeners, we learn that apparently Noonan had somehow been injured during the landing and was desperate to get out of the plane. Perhaps, the landing of the Electra in the very shallow water of the reef had also kicked up debris from the reef which had struck Noonan, or the violence of the landing and spray had caused injury, possibly even blown-out cockpit window(s) or a collapsed landing wheel and broken wing (the engine powering the radio on the other, intact wing).

The latter speculation is supported by the discovery of the image of an Electra landing wheel in the October, 1937 photo taken by Eric Bevington of the shipwreck from a distance of some 500 meters north and west of the wreck (near the northern tip of Gardner / Nikumaroro).

One line in Betty's notebook, "...she's going..." might be interpreted in the context of the surrounding listed remarks as either stating that the engine is running which seems unlikely since she is already broadcasting or, more plausibly, the flying duo's fear that the aircraft was slipping and being pulled by the rising tide and surf further out onto the reef.

The Electra landing wheel (enhanced) and revealed in the 1937 photo of the *Norwich City* taken by Eric Bevington probably came off during this rough landing or might be the remaining landing wheel that kept the engine clear of the surf until it too collapsed. I'm speculating as to this, but there it is in that photo and agreed by many aviation experts to be the landing wheel of an Electra. This might explain why Earhart could not or did not maneuver her aircraft as high onto the "beach" or away from the surf as possible (to minimize the effect of high tide). She did have "a broken wing" and most likely a collapsed landing gear under that wing.

That assumption also explains why Betty Klenck heard the panicky voices (especially Noonan's) speaking about the rising waters and wrote it down in her book or diary.

One can imagine the fear such relentless, rising water must have caused—to be sitting in one's tomb and faced with the imminent fate of the plane being dragged into the surf where drowning was a very real and frightening possibility, especially if they could see the edge of the reef not too far away. Especially so, if transmission was being performed at low-tide and in darkness. The duo landed there in daylight, at approximately 9:30 to10:00 a.m. local time as measured from Greenwich—approximately 4:00 to 4:30 PM in Florida at Betty Klenck's home.

For a duo that had just miraculously found a landing spot and respite, their desire to keep on preserving their lives and to be rescued were paramount. Fred Noonan's panic may be excused because he was injured somehow during the landing. Betty's notes do reveal a possible icy coolness as far as Earhart's remarks are concerned (said to Noonan while he rails at her), *"Will you help me?"* Noonan replies in the affirmative.

Read all these fragmentary conversations in "Betty Klenck's Notes" online and ask yourself if you agree with me. Ask yourself if Betty Klenck lied and was capable of making (all) this up? Ask yourself if these overheard Earhart broadcasts and details match the script of the *March of Time* radio-play broadcast in any respect? They do not. The script is available to read (7 pages) online. The radio-play broadcasts were made on July 8, 1937 and July 15, 1937. Note that this dramatic recreation of Earhart's last message is *after* the last, credible post-crash signal that was heard in the early morning of July 7. Betty Klenck's notes do stand up to scrutiny because I believe Betty was listening to the flyers right after they crash-landed on Gardner / Nikumaroro which was on the morning of July 2, 1937 at Gardner and about four to four-thirty pm in Florida. Frankly, I don't think Fred Noonan ever returned to the Electra cockpit after bailing that first day as tidal waters rose.

Let us further believe the statements and reports of seaplane fliers from the battleship *Colorado* and Commander Lambrecht who buzzed Gardner Island on July 9, 1937. And that not one of the six crew (pilots and observers) saw any Electra aircraft on the beaches or on that part of the exposed reef which was visible at the time per the tide level at the time of their observations. I will assume that, as the Colorado pilots flew toward the shipwrecked *Norwich City*, that view and associated debris was mostly all they looked at.

However, bear in mind, that that alone does not mean that the Electra wasn't there on the reef as you will see as you read further. It's entirely possible after a week on the reef that the Electra's remaining landing gear had collapsed, that the aircraft had been swept out further onto the reef, and the aircraft was submerged either in deeper water or by the height of the tide at the time the three aircraft from the *Colorado* flew by.

I will assert that the presence of the shipwreck—a total surprise to Lambrecht and his "seaplane posse"— was a distraction whenever they flew over that part of the reef. In fact, I'm asserting that throughout *time* after 1929, that shipwreck of the *Norwich City* was and has always been a distraction, and so were all the rusted bits and pieces of the ship that had broken off and washed up on the reef over the years which most everyone assumed were debris from the ship.

Where else could the 38 foot, three-inch-long, aluminum Lockheed Electra "hide" better than among the wreckage of this very ship or partially or completely submerged during high-tide, nearby? Especially if the wing extensions were torn off (see previous factory photos where such wing-extensions are removed during repairs). The size of the ship easily catches the eye and the lens of a handy camera at the time as the many historic pictures taken of the shipwreck through eight decades attest.

In fairness to the search party and those in charge of the search on the whole that July 8, 1937, they took note of the amateur and professional reports of post-crash signals allegedly made by Earhart and, obviously, took an interest in Gardner Island or Nikumaroro by sending the three seaplanes there to investigate on the following day, July 9, 1937.

Unlucky as to timing both for tides and for anyone alive after a week without adequate water? Fate? These men involved in the search did the best they could. As you are aware, hindsight makes it very easy for us to be critical. Time was against Earhart and Noonan. Considering the limitations of technology and both ship and aircraft speed at the time, I'm impressed with the

US Navy's 250,000 square mile search and the scope of it until the search ended on July 18. The cost? It had to have been staggering.

Then, I'm somewhat surprised that, in all this time since, no one else reported the images of the Electra I found in some of those aerial snapshots of the *Norwich City*. Especially so when confronted by spoken or anecdotal evidence from natives about "an airplane being visible at low tide," and "airplane parts washing up on lagoon beaches and turned into useful implements."

As for the Electra being submerged and out of sight, then why didn't the duo jump and wave from the beach when these three seaplanes purportedly "zoomed" over the island? It was *only* a week later. However, for survival limits, remember the "rule of threes:" three minutes without air, three hours in a hostile environment (extreme heat and cold), three days without water, and three weeks without food, each of which equals death.

Also, you must remember that Nikumaroro is an atoll several miles long with a central lagoon that is a mile wide. One has to walk around the island to get to the other side of the lagoon entrance or risk life crossing the lagoon entrance or walk the lagoon perimeter which is not continuous as to beach (while avoiding quicksand), and then try to penetrate through the dense vegetation to make it to the beach and ocean.

It is especially difficult if one has no boat to cross the lagoon. It's a long walk around this atoll or some fourteen kilometers. How long did these seaplanes buzz the island, and where? We know of only one photo of the island taken by the *Colorado* seaplanes posted a few pages ago and, ironically, it is of the opposite side of the island from the shipwreck. I'm sure there must be more photos, but they are lost or yet to be found.

The best place for "quick" access to both the ocean "beach" and lagoon for food like fish, crab, and turtles (narrowest passage) is the southern tip of the island. The shipwreck is on the northern part of the island. One can imagine a weakened duo of Earhart and Noonan desperately trying to guess where the seaplanes were heading or going to buzz next, or the aviators attempting to get through to the beach to be discovered only to see the seaplanes give up and fly away eastward. I've thought about these possible moments many times including both fliers waving futilely or both fliers dead from thirst and reclining under a tree where their bones were found by natives in 1940.

In July, temperatures at Gardner or Nikumaroro would be approximately 100 degrees Fahrenheit (36C) and very humid. Loss of water from our duo's bodies would be high. There is no fresh water source on the island except for what might be trapped in tree hollows after rainfall or in coconut milk. I've read that a prolonged drought was the condition there in 1937. Then, what provisions did the duo manage to bring ashore from the plane? What vital provisions had they sacrificed and left behind in Lae to save weight, the lack of which might easily have contributed to their demise? At best they had a few cans of Earhart's tomato juice and a couple of canteens of water?

Now, I want you to think about what might have possibly happened on that island they *allegedly* (for now) landed on between July 2, 1937 and the Navy seaplanes flyby on July 9, 1937? Think hard about *who* else might have shown up.

I've certainly dropped hints and clues for you in the narrative. And, thanks to my discoveries in vintage aerial photos, I'll prove to you that Earhart and Noonan did crash-land on Gardner Island on July 2, 1937 and they did not take off thereafter in the Lockheed Electra.

Or at least, I will try to convince you!

5

July 6, 1937

What is truth? How do you determine truth? In August 2022 as of this revision for an interview and blog to be held on August 12, some 85 years of speculation, theorizing, and discoveries of "new evidence" or interpretations of existing evidence have made the disappearance of Amelia Earhart and Fred Noonan on July 2, 1937 something of a skyscraper among the world's greatest "unsolved" mysteries involving a human(s) disappearance.

Many fail to understand the limits of certain technologies in those days when viewing matters with the lenses of the year 2022. At that time, we're only a decade post-Lindbergh flying the Atlantic solo in 1927 when Earhart attempts this final flying feat for a woman aviator.

For now, let us put aside over eight and a half decades of detective work by others and focus on a newspaper article that appeared in Melbourne, Australia on July 6, 1937 and a handwritten transcript of which is contained in the George Palmer Putnam papers at Purdue University.

Note that for the active searchers for Earhart and Noonan, across the dateline to the east, it was still July 5, 1937.

The article comes in two forms, the actual archive of the newspaper itself available online and a written transcript of said article probably used to transmit information by telegraph or wireless to other news services. Here below or on the next page is the online location of the handwritten transcript of said article. You can view both pages online at:

http://earchives.lib.purdue.edu/cdm/compoundobject/collection/earhart/id/2940/rec/30

Without any further information available to us, let us pretend we are searching for Amelia Earhart and Fred Noonan on or after July 2, 1937. Let us assume further that everything in this transcript / article is true and is the truth as people who reported it believed it to be true.

What stands out? On page one, we learn of the Pan Am direction bearing reported to *Itasca* and labelled as a "doubtful 213 degrees." We've shown that 213 degrees isn't doubtful when that bearing passes right by Nikumaroro or Gardner Island. We also learn that the Itasca has allegedly changed her course to the south on the basis of these reports of overheard post-crash radio signals from Earhart.

At the bottom of page one and onto page two, we learn that the *Itasca*, after she had changed course, picked up strong signals from "Mrs. Putnam" which stated "…she was on a reef south of the Equator."

Really? Where did this Aussie paper get these details? *Itasca* logs state that on July 2, they never heard anything further from Earhart after the word "Wait." Possibly the writer of this transcript or newspaper article here misattributed said statement to *Itasca*. Or that ship dismissed any further signals as hoaxes?

Now, let's back up a bit. According to the radiomen of the *Itasca* no new signals were received from Earhart after her last message at 8:44 (a.m.) on the morning of July 2, 1937. Now might this be semantics? A sanitized or clean log (the practice of making the log coherent and neat from the log notes made at the time of broadcasts)? Or is it the difference or a fine distinction between "*in-flight* radio signals" and "*post-downed-flight* signals?"

Let's put this discrepancy or ambiguity aside. One might ask, why not just disregard the conflicting statement in the transcript? One can't do that because a radio listener in Wyoming (Dana Randolph, 16) had reported per the Casper, Wyoming Tribune Herald on July 5, 1937) the same thing that had been reported in the Australian newspaper, and that he and father Cyrus and Uncle John had heard Earhart on the shortwave radio on July 4th say that she was *on a reef south of the Equator*. Another paper, *Rock Spring Rocket*, reported *something about a ship on the reef south of the Equator*. The latter may be enhanced or twisted because different newspapers reported slightly different words or ordering of the words: *reef, shipwreck, South* and *Equator*. Dana was unlicensed and the local police took the message for what it was. At least it made it into the newspaper forever preserving what I believe is the best and most accurate post-crash signal of where Amelia Earhart has landed: a reef south of the Equator with a shipwreck on it.

Yes, it's entirely possible that that young man's July 4th report from Wyoming made it to the wire services and is included in the July 6th newspaper article in Australia (note that due to the dateline, Wyoming's July 4 was probably Australia's July 5 or close to it). What's different from the Wyoming report of a broadcast is that the Australian newspaper attributed the message as being heard aboard *Itasca*. Maybe, that made it more "official" and newsworthy than the possible imagination of a sixteen-year-old?

Possibly, this information had been relayed to the searchers at the time. Note that confusion over names exists due to possible inaccuracies by reporters. Dana Randolph is referred to as the father of Charles Randolph in one article. The other article names Dana, father Cyrus, and Uncle

John. It's not relevant except as an arguing point. The Randolphs did report hearing Earhart on their shortwave. Per TIGHAR posts at https://tighar.org/smf/index.php?topic=1008.0 a check of the 1940 Census reveals father Cyrus, wife Betty, and son Dana Randolph, 18. I will add that it took a lot of courage for a Black family to come forward in 1937 and speak to the police about overhearing Earhart.

We've no way to cross examine these "witnesses." Dana Randolph apparently died in Los Angeles one researcher wrote. So, making a note of these "reports," let's move on.

The second page of this transcript of the newspaper article goes on to say that the *Itasca* was unable to get a bearing on those "strong signals" (Earhart's).

How much of this is actually true or truth? We've reached a stumbling block just three to four days into her disappearance. The discrepancy between two conflicting statements which were [the *Itasca* heard] "no further signals from Miss Earhart" in contrast to this hearsay statement in a newspaper that the *Itasca* heard that Earhart was "on a reef south of the Equator" and that *Itasca* had changed course in response to bearings found by both amateur and military radio operators in the Pacific. Well, we know the young Randolph heard these statements and reported them to the newspaper and police. How uncannily accurate!

Well, it's either true or partially true as subsequent events in our search will prove. In hindsight, Between Betty Klenck and Dana Randolph, *and believing them*, we have an excellent picture of what happened to Earhart and Noonan on July 2, 1937.

Let's assume the statements in this newspaper transcript are true. After all, three seaplanes were dispatched to search surrounding islands including Gardner

Island on July 9 (as soon as the USS *Colorado* arrived). Gardner sits at over four degrees south of the Equator.

So, where else might we look for corroboration? On July 4, 1937, a Wyoming adolescent of 16, Dana Randolph, reported hearing Earhart's voice saying they were *on a reef with a shipwreck south of the Equator*, or was it *ship wrecked on reef south of the Equator*? It's tempting to switch words around or emphasis to try to turn the word *ship wrecked* into *shipwreck* in order to bring the *Norwich City* into the picture. Would Earhart have referred to her Electra as a ship? Ambiguity isn't proof.

On the day she disappeared, July 2, 1937, an Amarillo, Texas housewife reported hearing Earhart's voice on the shortwave describing being *near or on a little island*. Others who claimed they overheard broadcasts by Earhart stated they heard her mention that Noonan was injured and needed immediate help.

Look, it is so easy to develop tunnel vision with minutiae and debate over exactly what Earhart said, what was overheard, and what was unclear, garbled, or misunderstood. What is important is that many reported hearing Earhart on those 3105 or 6210 frequencies. Assuming it was Earhart, then regardless of what was said by her, then Earhart is down, alive, and on land! The transmissions provide clues to her location. Certainly, the aerial photo image of her nearly intact airplane on Nikumaroro reef in 1940 helps corroborate what those radio listeners heard and reported in 1937.

Betty Klenck, age 15, heard Earhart and wrote down some of the same things as others had or similar phrases and statements (as if she heard one part while someone else heard another part of her broadcast). Noonan was frantic or so it seemed to Betty while she listened to Earhart's voice on her dad's shortwave radio in Saint Petersburg, Florida, and wrote excerpts of what was said in her notebook still available for all to see, here:

https://www.google.com/search?rlz=1C1ZCEB_enUS
850US850&sxsrf=ACYBGNTYdx1kmom1kZkYs-
yWVykStwDSsA:1571344089775&q=Betty%27s+notes&t
bm=isch&source=univ&sa=X&ved=2ahUKEwigyKnykKT
1AhVFjp4KHZOFDAkQsAR6BAgHEAE&biw=1536&bih
=750&dpr=1.25

Or you can view Betty's notes and a transcript of her handwriting, including her own commentary from an interview she gave about her notes and notebook to TIGHAR, here:

https://tighar.org/Projects/Earhart/Archives/Documents
/Notebook/notebook.html

Online, you can view the Tech-Times article quoting Ric Gillespie of TIGHAR and read about the people, including Dana and Cyrus Randolph who heard Earhart between July 2 and July 7, 1937, and what they heard said, here (some 57 credible post-crash radio signals):

https://www.techtimes.com/articles/232693/20180726/
amelia-earhart-s-desperate-calls-for-help-heard-in-radio-
distress-signals.htm

Noteworthy is the newspaper article from the Argus Melbourne Victoria (from which the transcript in the Putnam papers is derived and relied upon for this chapter) as it appeared in the newspaper, here, dated July 6th which mentions Earhart being on a reef:

https://trove.nla.gov.au/newspaper/article/11091405/58
2071

It's amazing what one can find online especially since this Australian newspaper ceased production and folded circa 1957.

To completely deny all of these "clues" as hoaxes, random speculation, attention-seeking teenagers, etc., requires one to call *everyone* a liar including the professionals who were listening in to those frequencies which Earhart used (Pan Am and the military). This denial of *all* witness statements is difficult to do when strangers, hundreds and thousands of miles apart, report hearing Earhart mention the "reef" and the "uninhabited island" "South of the Equator" and "Fred Noonan being injured" (*ship wrecked on reef*) whereby radio listeners inadvertently corroborated each other about what they had heard and reported. I'm reminded of the words *light housekeeping* versus *lighthouse keeping* in response to a verbal query of what type of work one does.

We are stuck with hearsay and all it's associated problems when it comes to evidence. Remember, some hearsay is permitted to be heard as evidence in court under a myriad of exceptions. But *we are not in court* as people seem fond of saying—a meaningless, gaslighting statement. We deal with credibility and corroboration and the preponderance of the evidence and make our decision based thereon.

To the many amateur radio reports of Earhart broadcasting, add the signals heard by Pan Am and the US military (all their bearings converging near Nikumaroro or Gardner Island), and one is hard pressed to call *everyone* either mistaken or liars. Then, remember this is 1937 with no internet; mass-media is radio and printed matter, and television is invented but not in widespread use though Hitler used it to broadcast a speech during the 1936 Olympic Games in Berlin, Germany.

I have found no independent corroboration that the *Itasca* heard what is reported in that Australian newspaper (or USA newspapers) and the transcript associated with it. But, taken together, a rather strong and compelling circumstantial case is being built, just three to four days after her airplane goes down, that Earhart and Noonan are alive, on land (reef), an island unknown to them, possibly injured, and desperate for rescue. Earhart's last alleged, post-crash signal heard on July 7 was: "*Can't last much longer....*" And no wonder on an island with no fresh water supply.

Remember, my armchair searchers, like the vintage 1960's TV show titled with the following words, "*You are There,*" you are there from July 2nd through July 9th, 1937 with no knowledge of the future.

These notes of Betty Klenck's were not made public at the time, but Betty and her father did report what she had heard to the Coast Guard. Obviously, her father thought enough of his daughter (or heard the radio signals and broadcasts himself) to dutifully make a report. Apparently, the report was brushed off. For our purposes, let us assume we had these notes from Betty as part of our package of data on July 6, 1937. The point is that these notes existed at the time. So, we will use them in our armchair search and rescue of Amelia Earhart. Do bear in mind the hearsay statement of Cyrus and Dana Randolph of Wyoming that corroborates Klenck and other overheard shortwave, post-crash signals from Earhart.

From Betty Klenck's notes, let's add "NY" or Betty's shorthand for what sounded like *New York City* (she said) and interpret that to be "*Norwich City*" in our armchair pursuit—the *shipwreck* (possibly) the teenage or young Charles Randolph spoke about in Wyoming to the Casper Tribune. Earhart said "it" many times per Betty's notes, which she said was "*New York or something like it.*" At least Dana Randolph heard and understood it to be a ship wrecked on reef South of Equator in the snippet of broadcast he overheard. I doubt Earhart was reminiscing about *The Big Apple* in her desperate broadcasts to reach anyone who might hear her. Furthermore, let's take a look at a list of numbers Betty wrote down in her notebook because she thought it might be a position. These are: "South 391065 Z or E."

Let's examine those numbers. As you're aware, you need two coordinates to establish a position—longitude and latitude. These numbers appear to be one coordinate, possibly latitude which makes no sense as is. Now, bearing in mind the sporadic reception of Earhart's broadcasts all the way to Saint Petersburg and to Betty's ear as evidenced in the partial phrases written down in her notebook, is it possible that Earhart gave a latitude position (the longitude numbers unheard in the ether) which Fred Noonan had taken using a sextant while standing on or near the reef?

If one assumes that the number of degrees south of the Equator also did not make it through the ether in this transmission by Earhart overheard by Betty or specifically, the possible missing, partial phrase "*4 degrees*" (39 minutes, and 10.65 seconds) was missed by Betty, isn't it an amazing coincidence that standing on the northern tip of Gardner / Nikumaroro at the reef edge, north of the shipwreck, using Google Earth as our tool, produces exactly that reading in minutes and seconds? The only number missing from that latitude coordinate is "4 degrees South!" So much for "random" numbers or Betty Klenck making them up. It is plausible that after hearing the words "4 degrees south" that Betty Klenck started writing down the rest of the numbers and forgot the number or phrase that started her writing actions.

Perhaps, this is a bit of a stretch? Yet, for Betty Klenck to imagine this number? It's akin to guessing most of the lottery numbers. And don't dismiss it as coincidence because Betty tells us it is Earhart speaking on the radio. So too does Dana, 16, father Cyrus, and Uncle John Randolph. And, as far as the accuracy of the rest of what Betty Klenck jotted down, her father respected her enough to go to the Coast Guard to inform them. Then, the father may have also heard Earhart, too. July 2 was a Friday and the Fourth of July weekend was ahead. Betty noted and wrote down some times on her notes, late afternoon times, but no dates. A six and a half to seven-hour difference in time zones puts Earhart on Nikumaroro sometime after 8.44 a.m. local time which would be approximately after 3:14 p.m. in Florida. If Earhart landed and was broadcasting at 0930 or 1000 hours locally at Nikumaroro, then Betty Klenck heard Earhart sometime between four to five p.m. EDT in Florida.

Instead, if this was Monday, July 5th and her dad had to work, did he arrive home in time to listen? Were these notes made on the weekend when her father was possibly home such as July 4th when the Wyoming teenager Dana Randolph said he had heard Earhart say something akin to "...*a wrecked ship on a reef south of the Equator*"? We don't know for certain. Certainly, on the holiday weekend, Betty's father had an opportunity to listen to the radio with his daughter. However, as concluded before, I believe Betty heard the first broadcasts right after Earhart's landing on Friday, July 2, 1937 circa four to five p.m. Florida time. Noonan, an injured and panicked Noonan, is still in the aircraft. An injured Noonan who probably couldn't physically get back into the aircraft, thereafter, or had no desire or will to do so. Read Betty's notes and transcriptions of what she heard. Does Noonan appear to be in despair and angry?

"Hey dad, it's Amelia Earhart on the radio!" Frankly, I would have said exactly that to my dad. Considering at a minimum that Betty's father had respected her enough to report what she heard to the US Coast Guard, it is not unreasonable to surmise that her father listened in as well. Remember that Betty also stated that her father had rigged additional antenna wire in their back yard to improve reception which explains why the neighbors could not hear the broadcast next door.

I recall a similar radio experience while in New Hampton, NH in 1964. We could not hear WABC radio from New York City on our AM radios by day and not too well at night but a fellow student, a radio enthusiast named Brad, strung an antenna to broadcast his own private radio station but, after complaints of interference, Brad strung an antenna for us around the patio or portico of the dorm building that also housed the school bell which allowed us to hook onto this new antenna and listen to WABC in NYC very clearly, day or night! I thought it miraculous!

I'm not aware of how accurate a hand-held sextant in 1937 could determine degrees, minutes, and *seconds* but even if Noonan took readings near the shipwreck, the margin of error which still keeps the minutes and seconds coordinates (which Betty wrote down) on the reef itself, per Google Earth, is remarkable. I remind you that the *March of Time* radio broadcast play about Earhart was on July 8 & July 15 (six days post disappearance), and nothing in that script matches anything that Betty Klenck wrote down except Earhart's radio call sign.

And yes, it could entirely be coincidence. But then, why is the "voice" of Amelia Earhart trying to convey those numbers and *"New York City?"* Why does a young Wyoming man report a "shipwreck" and Earhart's voice describing same and landing on a small island south of the Equator? Is Earhart telling us about a serial number from her plane? Her radio? A code? Hardly. We don't know, but the fact that it aligns with the minutes and seconds of a latitude coordinate for Nikumaroro should be telling enough and satisfying that we are on the correct track. But let's just be amused, interested, but not convinced by those numbers or the similar sounding shipwreck's name, or other coincidences spoken of by earwitnesses to radio broadcasts, *yet.*

Unfortunately, the record does not reveal any other listener who reported these overheard numbers or coordinates as recorded by Klenck although Dana Randolph comes close. One might imagine what a navigator or radio operator in the Navy would have made of such a number. The truth is, without the hindsight we have for Nikumaroro being at 4 degrees south latitude, any navy personnel would have been hard-pressed to guess Gardner Island or Nikumaroro at the time without all the evidence present *but not yet connected.* The minutes and seconds given (without the degrees N or S) could be *any* line of latitude within a reasonable distance of Howland Island.

Imagine if the Colorado seaplane pilots had heard about Dana Randolph and his describing to his father and Uncle, Cyrus and John Randolph, about Earhart mentioning a small island and a shipwreck on the reef's southern end? Yes, like the *Titanic* saga, we can generate quite a few "if only...." As well as generate the words or phrases we ourselves would have loved to have heard had we been tuned to our shortwave radios in July of 1937.

At the time, Betty Klenck's report was brushed off and ignored. The report by the Randolph family, per a newspaper report from the time, was relayed to authorities and searchers. Note the timeline which may or may not be related and might just be coincidence. Dana Randolph hears Earhart on Sunday July 4. It's reported in local newspapers on July 5 and 6th. An Australian paper carries information similar to what Dana Randolph reported on July 6, and by July 9 the seaplanes from the *USS Colorado* are buzzing Gardner Island and seeing the shipwrecked Norwich City.

It is unfortunate that Earhart and Noonan left no signal on the ground or had a signal fire to ignite. Without adequate water, hugging shade in hundred Fahrenheit or forty Centigrade heat and conserving energy, they did not think of any possibility of airplanes passing by the island in the middle of the Pacific. In 1937, Earhart's Electra was the sole aircraft on scene in that part of the world.

Again, Google Earth offers us another means of entertainment, and a way of participating in our armchair search and rescue of Amelia Earhart and Fred Noonan. I'm referring to Pan Am's Mokapu Point's radio direction finder and that "doubtful 213 degrees" bearing they gave on a purported post-crash Earhart radio signal.

Here's what you can do if you did not do so before: zoom in on Mokapu Pt. on Oahu located on the peninsula on the northeast shore (a triangular shape). Using the tools of the software, stick a yellow pin in it. Then, zoom out and find Nikumaroro or Gardner Island. Zoom in as close as you can and stick a pin on the reef right near the bow of what remains of the shipwrecked *Norwich City*. Zoom out and use the tools once more to establish a line with navigation turned on, and then click to start the line at Mokapu Point in zoom-in mode; then, zoom out and extend that line to Nikumaroro / Gardner; zoom in and attach it to the pin near the bow of the shipwreck. Now, what was your bearing on that line you just drew? How many degrees? Did you get approximately 212 degrees (211.6)? Are you impressed?

What's so *doubtful* about Pan Am's reported bearing of 213 degrees, now? We're using a modern, computer tool but it is no different than extending a bearing line on an appropriate (possibly, highly inaccurate) chart in 1937. That line or bearing Pan Am gave as a "doubtful 213 degrees" is almost on the money and passes right by Gardner Island to the exclusion of others within the range of Howland Island, Earhart's destination.

Several bearings from listening stations on Oahu, Midway and other places all intersect near Gardner / Nikumaroro. Even Robert Ballard is impressed and mentioned this evidence in the recent NG TV broadcast as rather convincing, and which cannot be ignored or dismissed by us, either.

Now, add to this the reported words heard by radio listeners, "We're on a reef south of the Equator... on an uninhabited island... New York City (*Norwich City*)." Then, taking several "radio earwitnesses" as a whole, coupled with the bearing given by Pan Am and other military operators listening on that same frequency, including many Japanese listeners, there's little doubt that they detect *some* signal on the wavelengths, 6210 and 3105, used by Earhart including her call sign emanating or propagating from the area around Gardner / Nikumaroro Island, in the Phoenix chain.

At the time, **whom** else could it be? Gardner Island was uninhabited. And, whom else (besides *Itasca*) was broadcasting on that special frequency in the middle of the Pacific Ocean other than Amelia Earhart (and Noonan)?

From memory, I also recall that all these radio messages from Earhart overheard across the Pacific, the USA, and Canada, and their broadcast times actually coincided with low tide at the reef on Gardner / Nikumaroro. I believe Ballard also mentioned this in the NatGeo *Expedition Amelia* broadcast and commented that such evidence was difficult to ignore. This is further, compelling evidence that the plane is on the reef and Earhart has to use low tide to run the engine such that the propeller clears the surface of the water and charges the radio batteries that feed power to the radio. The reef at Nikumaroro is nearly always awash but the depth varies according to the tides, the time of year, and the lunar and solar tides.

Remember that everything mentioned so far is true and exists. Earhart is still alive and could have been rescued if only someone had put the pieces together in time—sadly, that's exactly what is said about the terror attacks of 9/11.

Presumably, after believing in and viewing the Electra in the June, 1941 aerial photo some 600 meters south and east of the landing wheel photographed in October, 1937, we must accept that the wreckage was consistently in motion at every tide cycle, two high and two low tides over a 24 hour and fifty-minute period, which saw the Electra slowly dragged into deeper water (...*she's going!*"). Then, according to the Tech-Times article that quotes TIGHAR sources, Earhart's last known, credible broadcast was in the early (wee) hours of July 7 (*This is Amelia Earhart. Can anyone hear me?*). That's five to six days of post-crash radio signals from July 2. If this is truth and to be believed, then we have to assume that the Electra became submerged on the reef due to the collapse of its remaining landing gear (or the batteries died, or the plane exhausted its fuel) sometime between July 7 and the arrival of the *Colorado's* seaplanes on July 9 who reported neither seeing the Electra aircraft nor any survivors trying to attract their attention from the beaches.

This lack of seeing survivors, if true and from a proper altitude from which they might have been seen, has several possible conclusions: 1. Earhart & Noonan perished from thirst between July 7 and July 9, which I find unlikely but possible; 2. Earhart and Noonan had become so weak from dehydration in the near hundred degree temperatures and humidity that they are either unconscious, delirious, or too weak to make it to the beach area from their assumed shady spot in the vegetation, palm trees, or other trees, including weakly trying to guess exactly where those airplanes would buzz at low altitude; and 3. Could it be that Earhart and Noonan are *no longer on the island* when the seaplanes arrive on July 9?

Oh! I can hear every Japanese-capture theorist sit up.

Recall when I asked you to think hard about why this duo were not seen on the island during the flyby by the Navy seaplanes on July 9? Now, who or who might have "rescued" them and taken them off the island? Some mystery naval or fishing vessel?

While you're thinking, read on.

Remember the survival story of famed WWI ace Eddie Rickenbacker from 1942? Who were they successfully avoiding while drifting in the ocean? They successfully avoided being seen by Japanese patrol ships! Yes, it was wartime in '42 but remember that on July 9, 1937 the Japanese manufactured an incident to justify their invasion of China when it was still July 8th at Gardner Island. Japan was also secretly and very actively preparing for war, and most anxious to keep this a secret from the United States as National Archive documents attest (discussed later). Otherwise, why lay the keel of the mighty battleship *Yamato* on November 4, 1937 at Hiroshima in total secrecy, and just four months after Earhart disappeared if not for commitment to total war with the United States?

More about this, shortly. Do keep reading as two major surprises are next. For those of you who support other theories about her disappearance and death, I can only ask for your patience, and to see this work to the end. I have not forgotten you!

So, my armchair search and rescue team, consider that I place at your disposal in a sci-fi sense, every 21st century piece of technology including planes, ships, satellites and the like, for our look back at these events. Wouldn't you have "zoomed" in on Gardner Island on or before July 6, 1937 (July 5 depending upon which side of the dateline you're on) based upon the evidence presented so far?

Had these technological miracles existed then, what do you think a satellite view of the reef area around the shipwrecked *Norwich City* would have revealed at <u>low tide</u> between July 2 and July 6 (5th), 1937, assuming Earhart's last radio broadcast was July 7?

Bingo! You would have seen the Lockheed Electra still highly visible on the reef because it was transmitting radio signals up to the early morning on July 7th.

Now, you ask me, *how could I (you) know this for certain?*

Read on and I'll show you.

6

The Plane! Where is the Electra?

Did you spot the airplane in those old black and white aerial photos, yet? I added more photos to not leave you guessing for too long. So far, most followers of the Amelia Earhart disappearance have been treated to numerous claims by TIGHAR and what that group term "The Nikumaroro Hypothesis." Over a dozen TIGHAR expeditions, two ocean searches, including Robert Ballard's recent quest in August 2019, have turned up not a single, <u>verifiable</u> part of Earhart's Electra aircraft. No aluminum from the plane was found by Ballard despite all of his impressive equipment and reputation for finding sunken ships like Titanic, Bismarck, and PT-109.

It was not Dr. Ballard's fault!

To be fair, it took Robert Ballard and several, repeated expeditions to find those historic shipwrecks mentioned. Ballard plans on returning to Nikumaroro in 2022 (pandemic-pending) or 2023 should more evidence of Earhart landing there be forthcoming. As for coming up empty this past August 2019, that is not Doctor Ballard's fault. He was somewhat "misled" by the photo of the Electra landing wheel (Bevington photo), and by TIGHAR's Ric Gillespie's repeated mantra that the "Electra slipped off the reef" in the vicinity of said landing wheel.

I'll *repeat* that endlessly repeating what was total speculation in the first place does not magically change original speculation into fact. Ballard found nothing for good reason as you will see. An earlier, downscaled version of such an underwater search by TIGHAR for

Earhart's aircraft or parts thereof in the location of that landing wheel had also produced nothing offshore but speculative targets.

What has been found over time on the island have been skeletal remains, shoes, Cat's Paw heels, broken liniment bottles, freckle cream jars (pots), cosmetics, a broken pocketknife, zipper-pull, lighter, and other detritus which have all been attributed to Amelia Earhart despite the fact that, starting in 1938, the island was re-inhabited by natives until 1963 including English officials and women. Additionally, WWII years saw Americans operating a radio and relay station on the southern tip of the island.

Add to this "crowd" of new native inhabitants, the several expeditions from New Zealand and Great Britain for possible runway use, tree and coconut production, and the USA occupying the southern tip during WWII, you end up with hundreds of tramping feet both native and Anglo-European including their associated trash. I'm not saying that all found objects are not Earhart's, I'm simply pointing out how difficult it is to tie any of these to her with any certainty.

In hindsight though, since I can prove the Electra was on the reef on Nikumaroro / Gardner in three photos taken during the period 1938-1942, I do give some credence to the "Freckle cream" jar, zipper piece, and lady's compact glass and rouge powder that TIGHAR members found on the island. Well done! I still hold out hope that both her briefcases or what is left of them will be found.

After all, if an Electra aircraft wreck is on the island, the only Electra in the vicinity in 1937 also contained Fred Noonan and Amelia Earhart. Four photos now comprise evidence in support thereof: from Bevington's 1937 photo catching a landing wheel in the shallows at reef's edge, to the three photos I will once more present shortly, taken 1938, 1941, and1942.

There is even controversy about the shoe size reportedly found in 1940 along with the partial skeleton. Earhart supposedly wore a US 6½ shoe. In those days, and from very narrow shoes purportedly purchased in Ireland by her in 1932, a ten-inch length translated into a 6.5 size shoe. It wasn't a "size ten shoe" but a shoe ten inches in length that was found. A reasonable (mis-) interpretation but pundits point to the "wrong" shoe size as "proof" Earhart was not the owner of the shoe found on Gardner Island in 1940 alongside the human bones that Gerald Gallagher reported (and kept secret) at the time.

Gallagher was in charge of the resettlement of Gardner Island at the time and the National Geographic special "Expedition Amelia" mentioned Gallagher's telegram stating that the bones might be the remains of Amelia Earhardt (*sic* – no "d" in Earhart). Noteworthy is the lack of any mention of Fred Noonan by Gallagher.

But other than record this in our armchair pursuit and be amazed at another possible piece of the historical record regarding Earhart's disappearance, we needn't dwell on the shoes as you will soon see.

Then, there are those bones or human skeletal remains found in 1940 by Gallagher and sent to Suva, Fiji. The bones were subsequently identified as a male and an islander of unknown inhabitation date. The then doctor's findings that it was a male in his forties or fifties are discredited decades later because he was not a forensic expert. Nevertheless, the bones are lost in the mists of time due to WWII until someone states they have traced the bones to Tarawa, and skull fragments are being tested for DNA as I write this (inconclusive due to advanced deterioration). Personally, I believe the skull piece was Fred Noonan while the rest of the 5'6" skeletal remains were Earhart's remains. I call it a forensic, *chimera* postmortem of two sets of remains treated as one.

The original forensic report from 1940, later disputed in modern times, and using the notes and measurements from the same doctor's notes found in England by TIGHAR, a modern forensic study of just those measurements and photos of Earhart concludes the bones are of a European female, their measurements matching probably Earhart. Then, this finding is also strongly disputed by other, modern forensic experts.

So far, there's nothing definitive, and the only hope is that DNA can be found in these old bones and a mitochondrial DNA comparison made to known living relatives of Amelia Earhart—a niece (I'm not sure about Noonan or any bones attributable to him or DNA testing of any Noonan relative, who have never been identified).

We lawyers are familiar with the "battle of the experts" as testimony from them is elicited to win over a jury. This process is both tedious and wearisome to judges and juries. My law school Dean characterized this battle of the experts in his affected, Texas accent as "the risk of *non-persuasion*."

Yes, my law school dean did make a lasting impression on me. I had two classes with him in my first year, and his affected accent and inflections were humorous though he taught the law well.

Per "Expedition Amelia," the DNA provided from the skull fragment found on Tarawa is severely deteriorated, unreadable, and no mitochondrial match is possible to existing relatives. Also, analysis of the assembled skull fragments, though female, are quite unlike European skulls and the chances of it being a European female are low per the expert examining the fragmented skull.

I assume that the bones and their paper trail led to Tarawa but not to a specific box or locale.

Robert Ballard went to search Nikumaroro because he believed in the enhanced photo image of an Electra landing wheel found in a 1937 photograph taken by Eric Bevington who explored the island in October of that year just three months after Earhart disappeared. Robert Ballard stated he went around the island to various depths of 600 to 900 meters but found no trace or a single piece of aluminum from the Electra airplane.

Ultimately, we have the aluminum fragment found on the island more than twenty years ago by TIGHAR. It's been tested, analyzed, speculated about, and attributed to the aluminum patch installed on the Electra window in Miami during Earhart's second attempt to fly around the world. Now, the forgotten wire attached to that aluminum fragment is seeing new thoughts and more speculation.

Unfortunately for TIGHAR, the ALCLAD markings and the "AD" and another, "faint D" on the aluminum piece found make this patch appear to be manufactured well after Earhart's disappearance. The piece has been denounced as a part of a WWII plane, a shelf, and other non-Earhart origins.

Frustrating, isn't it? As Ballard remarked, "One piece of the plane and we have the whole thing."

I believe that I have discovered the "whole thing" in three vintage photos.

The Lockheed Electra was 38 feet, 3 inches in length. The Norwich City had a beam (width) of 53.5 feet. A lot of metal was in that all-aluminum plane along with two mighty and heavy Pratt & Whitney "Wasp" engines to turn the propellers.

Despite over a dozen expeditions, sifting of soils, searching below ocean water, and surveying the atoll by drone, not one further identifiable piece of Amelia

Earhart's Lockheed Electra has ever been found on Gardner / Nikumaroro Island or in the ocean on the submerged reef down to depths of 900 meters. Robert Ballard even surveyed the ocean floor but turned up nothing from the Lockheed Electra, but ironically found a hat blown off the head of one of his crew which had sunk to the bottom.

However, natives later settled on Gardner / Nikumaroro during 1938-1963 did anecdotally speak about "airplane parts" that washed up in the lagoon which were used to make implements during the time the island was colonized, and of the "plane" on the reef visible at low tide. But not one direct photo, not one salvaged piece or "turned into implement" piece of aluminum from such airplane parts survives.

It's maddening!

Critics of TIGHAR and of others who believe in this "Nikumaroro hypothesis" point to this lack of parts from a large airplane as proof that the whole theory is bunk. The unsuccessful Ballard quest has them hooting and jeering with glee. Some critics even go as far as to vehemently call the previous "finds" and "data" deliberate lies manipulated by the Director of TIGHAR, Ric Gillespie, strictly to raise funds and donations to the organization to sustain his large, annual Director's salary.

Lies? No. Some misperceptions and preconceived notions? That is more likely. Surprise! TIGHAR is correct about Earhart crash-landing on Nikumaroro, or Fred Hooven, the originator of the Nikumaroro hypothesis, is correct.

Such criticisms and personal attacks do not address the science and discoveries. So, is the Nikumaroro hypothesis, or theory or scenario, bunk or not? The great Robert Ballard finds nothing! No aluminum from a plane, whatsoever! A TIGHAR wild goose chase! So, it must be true then that the "Nikumaroro Hypothesis" is bunk" right?

No, wrong! The Nikumaroro hypothesis is true. You'll see why, shortly.

Based on finding nothing in the form of aluminum wreckage might lead one to conclude the plane isn't there because one believes the plane never landed there on Gardner Island on July 2, 1937. **Except**, I can see the plane on the reef at Gardner / Nikumaroro in three vintage aerial photographs, one from 1938, 1941, and the other from 1942.

There, especially in the 1941 photograph, is an object that is light-colored (aluminum) blending into the background, surrounded by debris and the overwhelming presence of the shipwrecked *Norwich City*, which is the unmistakable nose portion of the Electra including cockpit windows, missing nose hatch, wing-stubs, and round shadows of one, possibly both engine nacelles, or bare firewalls.

Despite TIGHAR posting on their website that high resolution scans of these Nikumaroro photos were being made available to members, no one has ever noticed the Electra aircraft (or published about it) before as far as I can tell, and no one went looking for that self-same debris in other photos until I did, finding the plane in a 1942 photograph then further up-reef. A subsequent search found the telltale nose rather blurrily peeking out of the surf in a 1938 photo north and east of the shipwreck—on the other side, the port side of the shipwreck!

As to the 1938 photo, if that was all I had, a blurry, small image on the brink of pixelization, I'd nod my head at assertions of "illusion" and wishful thinking. Except that this same image, the same shadow configuration (cockpit windows and open nose hatch) and light-color (aluminum presumably), is prevalent and visible in all three photos taken in <u>three different years,</u> and the three images I found are in <u>three different locations</u> on the reef.

The Electra may have ceased flying but it did not stop moving along the reef as if drawn to the shipwreck like a magnet.

My high school friend Patrick S. and I graduated in 1968. He went on to serve in the US Army in Vietnam where he served in intelligence and photo analysis with the 199th. I showed him the image in the 1941 photograph and the enlargement I had made of the Electra aircraft at the starboard stern of the shipwreck. I also showed him the other photos posted online and herein which show and help orient the eye to Electra features in the image if you know where to look for it, and if you are able to instantly recognize the distinctive nose of the Electra like I did.

I informed Patrick S. that I had been dismissed outright by TIGHAR when I posted my findings in their Forum and was subsequently locked out of the thread with cries of "illusion created by water and the reef" and other remarks akin to seeing Jesus in the clouds or in a tree cutting or potato chip shape.

My friend Patrick took his time, and these are his written remarks to me and his opinion concerning the 1941 photo:

"Size and shape is definitely a man-made object. Just how many times do you see an X-shape occur in a natural setting? Shadows confirm the likelihood of a non-natural object. The object in question casts a shadow in the same angle and direction of the other objects in the photo. And the shadow is a slightly lighter degree of darkness as you would expect it to be in shallow water as indicated by the waterline running left to right. The shadows along the bottom of the object are heavier along the bottom and left side, indicating the

object has dimension and is not a reflection or color shading. And, the color sure looks like aluminum to me. Especially when compared to the darkness of color of the corroded ship's color and the dark color of the nearby debris from the ship. As for setting, it definitely is out of place and shouldn't be there. I totally concur with your assessment. A very good job by an untrained image interpreter. Well done, you are right."

I don't have any further expert resources to go to. My request that the photos be sent for analysis by TIGHAR were laughed at and dismissed by Ric Gillespie. Due to that and other hostile treatment, I resigned from TIGHAR after being a member for only a few weeks.

A discovery that would help prove TIGHAR's Nikumaroro hypothesis, no less! Does that mean that such proof that the Electra is on the reef in those vintage photos might mean the end of the Earhart quest by TIGHAR? Only someone like Robert Ballard and his resources and funding can find that plane today. How does all of that affect interest, membership, and donations to TIGHAR? Hmm…. Just a thought.

You can find the 1941 photo online here for your own perusal and blowup on whatever software you wish:

https://tighar.org/Projects/Earhart/Archives/Research/Bulletins/80_LongFarewell/1941NC.jpg

Here is the June, 1941 photo with the Electra circled (it may be on following page depending on your Kindle settings):

I invite you to copy the image online onto software such as "Paint" and slowly enlarge the photo. Can you see why it was never noticed? An enlargement is presented below. The aircraft is practically camouflaged by the surroundings and its location, and by the quality of the reproduced image in whatever medium you are looking at. Vary your distance according to your eyesight and correction for either distance of closeness. Can you see the plane as "plain as day" in the above photo? Well, no one noticed the Electra image in this photo for some 80 years.

Below is an enlargement of the object. Clearly, within the circle at lower left is the nose shadow (nose hatch gone), cockpit windows shadows, and fuselage of the distinctive Electra present. At the rear / top of this image, is that an upside-down tail assembly visible?

In this June, 1941 photo, the Electra has spent nearly four years on the reef, usually partially or wholly submerged at high tide, both its landing gear probably shorn off as well as a portion of the center fuselage and tail boom either broken off or twisted. The arrow points to a circular shadow which corresponds to an engine firewall in the correct location just like the Lockheed repair photos previously shown. The nose hatch hole is obvious; the hatch is missing.

The Electra has followed the general debris flow and the longshore drift just "offshore", moving south and east, and has made its way past the bow of the

Norwich City where it has washed up in the low-tide shallows in the lee of the shipwreck for this miracle photo taken at the right time, right tidal condition, and the right place and altitude above the shipwreck.

Notice the surf action at the stern of the ship. The previous wave has ebbed, joined the incoming wave, and the Electra is revealed in that brief moment of quietude! I remarked to a friend that it is as if a deity had said, "take that photo now!"

For your perspective, the light-colored object has a large, circular shadow at the nose, a shadow produced by the hole in the nose because the nose-hatch has come off. Slightly above the nose hole are the cockpit windows. The image has what appears to be wing stubs (overall X shape) out to just beyond the engine nacelles. An inboard, port wing shadow seems to indicate the presence of an engine nacelle, possibly the Pratt & Whitney "wasp" engine is still attached. Further to the rear, it appears the plane has partially broken just aft of the trailing edge of the wings (the twisted tail of the Electra may still be partially attached here but it is difficult to tell). It might also be backward further up-reef if you scrutinize a light-colored object above the Electra and think it is the tail section from behind.

To improve your perspective, I again include the following photographs of Earhart's Electra undergoing repairs at Lockheed after her ground loop crash in March of 1937. Note Amelia's smile as she poses in the nose hole and study the alignment and relationship of the cockpit windows. Then, see the photos below of the port-and starboard views of the Electra at the factory to better orient your eyes to the object in the 1941 photograph.

Below, this is a port view of the Electra with port engine nacelle and firewall removed. Note the starboard firewall (round) still attached. Note large nose-hole.

Doesn't this photo angle nearly mimic the angle of the object in the 1941 photo of the shipwreck above, and which bears an identical appearance? Note the overall large size of the nose hole here in the above factory photo which is consistent with the large, circular shadow at the nose of the aircraft object in the June 1941 photo of the shipwreck and reef.

Below is a picture of the starboard side of the Electra under repair so that you can see the starboard engine nacelle. It is my belief that, on the reef in the surf and waves, the heavier Pratt &Whitney wasp engines (visible in the Ford Island crash photo) possibly detached and were washed further down the reef to the south and east, being heavier, more compact, with less surface area for the waves, currents, and flowing water to act upon. Anecdotally, the island native who stated he found an engine on the reef and salvaged it sticks out in my mind.

However, in the below-posted 1942 photo on page 97 of this 6X9 manuscript, the starboard engine nacelle seems unusually large in shadow possibly indicating that the "wasp" engine is still attached there, although it is a large, round hole to begin with. Either way, it's inconclusive but definitive of the Electra itself.

Also, it is likely that the wing portions not yet installed in the above photo would fail, and then break away from water, wave, and surf action over time especially with the Electra resting on its wings and belly. Note the tapering of the under-fuselage which would make the nose rise slightly if the plane were flat on its fuselage with landing gear gone or collapsed. That is precisely the pose or angle of the nose in the subsequent 1942 photo of the reef and shipwreck taken in January 1942 (possibly on next page). Note arrow pointing to possibly the aluminum tail section reversed and upside down 180 degrees, above fuselage and nose wreckage, and also note the circular, starboard firewall shadow near hand-drawn arrowhead that is precisely the location for it relative to the nose of the plane shown. The larger arrow points to the open nose hatch hole.

Yes! As difficult as it is to believe, unnoticed for 80 years, there is the Lockheed Electra on the reef at Gardner / Nikumaroro, hiding in plain sight in an aerial photograph taken June 1941, and January 1942, unnoticed, and "hidden" so to speak by all the ship debris and the overwhelming presence of the hulking ship itself, so frequently eye-catching and photographed by practically every visitor to the island.

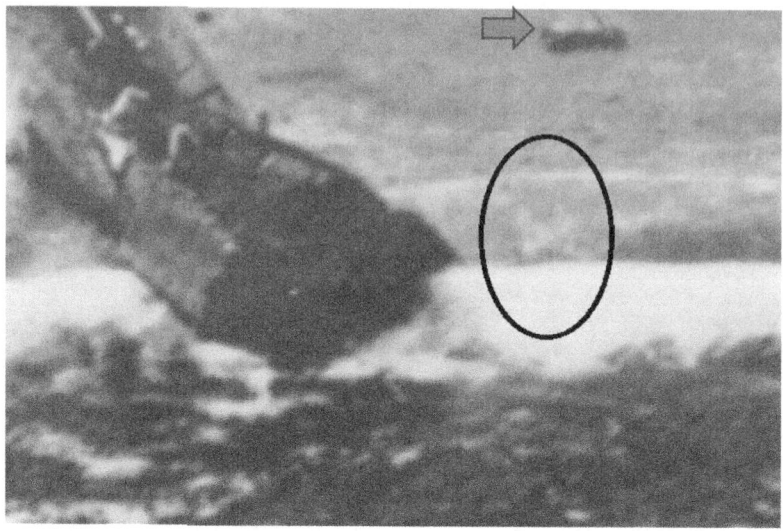

We have the good fortune that this photo was taken at low tide, at the right angle, and the correct altitude. This is one of those miracle photos of a scene that only occurs twice every 24 hours and 50 minutes and not necessarily in daytime. And, considering the odds, a definite miracle photo taken that day in June 1941. Note the blue arrow points to that shiny aluminum, triangular shape that this fuselage debris will join in the January 1942 photo six months after this photo was taken. Can you clearly see the angled leading edges?

Additionally, my friend Patrick S., the former US Army Intelligence photo analyst, asked me if it is my opinion that in the 1941 photo the twin-tail of the Electra may still be intact at this point judging by the length of the light-colored object and what may be a very blurry tail boom with two small uprights (rudders) still attached.

It's a long shot, but it is possible but I'm unable to tell at this resolution and with the limited tools at my disposal. It does appear so, but the fuselage's apparent length seems short to me though the tail boom could be twisted and therefore "throwing the eye off" as to the Electra's proportions lengthwise. That tail boom, or part of it, may also be up-reef a short distance away as previously mentioned judging from the shiny triangular or trapezoidal shape of the rear, horizontal stabilizer.

Some (including TIGHAR) have argued that the "scale is all wrong" and that the image I've discovered is too big compared to the ship with a beam of 53.5 feet. My response was that I had anticipated that question and had measured the Electra image. The actual, full-size Electra at 38 feet three inches in length could fit nose to tail abeam of the ship and still have 15 feet to spare. Measuring both in the photograph, discounting the difference in height from the deck to the water's surface, The Electra scale fits rather easily alongside the scale of the *Norwich City* with room to spare including adding to its length for my presumed, missing tail piece.

As to cries of "illusion," I answer that with, *does an illusion move*? Here, below, seven months later in a January 1942 photo of the *Norwich City*, the same debris has moved up-reef to lie off the starboard bow of the ship with the nose (nose-hole) facing the waterline of the ocean (a consistent feature and orientation in all three photos). It is also this photo that gives possible credence to the fact that the starboard "wasp" engine is still attached to the nacelle due to its large shadow.

The tail boom appears to be still "with" or in proximity to the airplane although the lighter part of this image visible above the fuselage does have a curved or "angled" leading edge of the possible port side of the horizontal stabilizer facing 180 degrees away. This might indicate that there has been separation of the two parts since the 1941 photo was taken seven months before.

In this 1942 photo, the same nose-hole and cockpit windows shadows, and even the slight rearward cant of the fuselage is evident and the latter attributable to the design of the Electra and the tapered fuselage, rearward. Might that be the lighter-color tail boom turned 180 degrees above it? Difficult to tell but those shapes are not natural, and they are not rusty, either.

Note that the wreckage circled does not appear in this position in the earlier June 1941 aerial photo. From the angle from its last position seven months earlier to its position here, it would appear that the Electra is continuing on its way south and east and possibly headed for the lagoon channel nearby, some several hundred meters distant as evident in this (same) photo not enlarged below.

Seems the Electra wreckage is destined for the lagoon.

Intrigued by these two finds, I wondered if there might be earlier aerial photos of the *Norwich City*. I found one from 1938. A hunt for the telltale nose of the Electra with a similar, large nose-hole and cockpit windows as dark shadows on a light background paid off. I found such an image to the north and west of the wreck (on the other or port side of the shipwreck) which was also in the surf-line, and which is difficult to discern (see circle in surf to the left or port side of the shipwreck below).

Here below is the best enlargement of the 1938 image that I'm capable of making. It's extremely blurry, tiny, and at the limit before pixelization overly-dominates an enlarged image. You must vary your distance from the picture (especially in the paperback version), depending upon your eyesight and correction, possibly closing one eye, until you see the relatively tiny dark nose of the Electra peering at you in the same configuration of nose-hole shadow and cockpit-windows (eyes) shadows like in the other two photos—the "dog face" of the Electra's nose. Uncannily consistent, isn't it? With the eBook, you can manipulate the photo yourself.

Be grateful that we have these incredibly lucky photos with their hidden information. An enlargement appears below.

The arrow points to the large nose hatch hole; the dark cockpit windows shadows are visible just above it. This is the best I can do in this medium and from copying that image into the manuscript and then onto Amazon. You may be as skeptical as you want but it is the only link between Bevington's magic landing gear in a 1937 photo and the aerial photos of the fuselage on the starboard side that I have presented. These photos comprise my so-called *four frame movie* that documents the transition of the Electra from that broken-off landing wheel some 700-750 meters south and east to the starboard stern of the *Norwich City*.

Note that the tide and the surf-line is a long way up-reef and past the stern of the shipwreck and closer to the bow than it is in the 1941 photo where the surf-line is at the broken-off stern. The ship is 397 feet or 122 meters long though a large portion of the stern broke off in 1938 but not yet in this photo though the back of the ship is broken, and the stern sits on the reef here. In this photo the Electra is approximately one ship-length away from the port side of the Norwich City. The future journey from this moment, December 1, 1938, to June 1941 is 2.5 years to make it past the bow of the shipwreck, and to rest in the lee of the shipwreck in June, 1941 for the definitive image captured on film.

I'm inserting the following image during a June 2021 revision. My reason is my discovery that the photo is at the earliest January 30, 1939 when the New Zealand survey team arrived at Gardner / Nikumaroro. Reading Gilbert's reports, previous captioning of "1938" for the photo by others has proven erroneous. Although the NZ expedition commenced in late 1938, they didn't get to Gardner / Nikumaroro until 1/30/1939. Take a look to the starboard of the ship (the photograph's left) in the water. See that horizontal, straight gray line above the water level at photo's left edge? See that dark shadow in what looks to be an aluminum fuselage piece? See the *arch* shape in the upper part of that dark shadow? I believe it is the (non-rusted) aluminum fuselage of the Electra with the open cabin door on the port side presented, and possibly a window in the fuselage further to the edge. I further believe that it is the tail section or rather the aircraft from behind the wings back to the tail section that has made it here at this date because it is lighter.

It is consistent with what we see of the additional shiny wreckage seen a short distance from the Electra in the astonishing June 1941 photo presented previously, and which the Electra eventually joins in the January, 1942 photo. Note that this would be the earliest that I can document the Electra, or the aft part of it, being on the starboard side of the shipwreck after a journey of some 700 meters from the location of the landing wheel or Bevington Object photo to port or the other side of the shipwreck.

The Bevington object (Electra landing wheel) in the 1937 photo (see many examples online & below) is over 400 meters from the ship's port side in the 1937 photo. So, by the time this January 30, 1939 photo was taken, the Electra had traveled approximately 250 meters or about 1000 feet south by east toward the shipwreck. By June of 1941, the Electra has passed the ship (presumably by the bow) and is in the shallows on the starboard side near the stern in the previous photo.

Quite a journey!

Below is the 1937 Bevington photo made famous by TIGHAR with inset showing blowup of object sticking up above the water. The "Y" or "V" shaped yoke is distinctive as well as the round tire.

Well, isn't that stunning?

As for the three photos I present of the Electra fuselage and nose sections in the surf and up-reef, unless you believe that three different locations on the reef, in different years, and in different tidal conditions, can produce the same "illusion" then we have evidence that the Electra did a tidal dance on the reef, near the precipitous edge of the reef, four times a day (24 hrs 50 min for four tides) while it moved closer and closer to the shipwreck and eventually ended up on the other side of the shipwreck as seen in the June 1941 aerial photo.

That is amazing.

From the time Earhart landed the Electra here on Gardner / Nikumaroro on July 2, 1937 the ocean waves, currents, prevailing water and debris flow, and four tides per day, washed the Electra up-reef, down-reef a little bit each day (an average of 18 inches or 46 centimeters daily) but miraculously and fortunately the tides never pulled this large part of the plane wreckage off the reef and into the depths as late as January, 1942 when our (my) photographic evidence ends.

After watching the National Geographic Special "Expedition Amelia" just a few minutes ago (2019) and the emptiness and the lack of one single piece of aircraft aluminum that Ballard failed to find north and west (port) of the wreck is perhaps explained by my photos— the Electra wasn't washed into the ocean depths in the so-called "target area" of the Bevington object or Electra landing wheel in the 1937 photograph. The Electra journeyed some 500 meters or more in four years and appears to be continuing that journey in the January, 1942 aerial photo, at an average speed of 46 cm a day.

Seeing the sheer drop-off of the reef during the TV special which was displayed on Ballard's equipment, it is nothing short of miraculous that the Electra somehow managed to work its way down the reef to the south and east until it reached the shipwreck itself and passed it presumably by the bow and then washed down to the surf line seen in the June, 1941 photo.

The reef profile does have a dip and up-curl near the edge which I attribute to what saved the Electra from washing off the reef at that landing wheel location in the 1937 photo.

Then, when it arrived there at the shipwreck by tidal action, the Electra must have been continuously washed against the port side of the shipwreck in the accumulated swell caused by the ship blocking the flow of the waves and water. This welled-water and its momentum, inhibited by the shipwreck's bulk, forced or pushed the plane up-reef and past the port bow where water flow pushed it beyond the wreck. Now (then), with the Electra clear of the bow, the waves and water flow picked it up and we see the Electra near the starboard stern area in the 1941 photo. Here, in the starboard lee of the shipwreck, the Electra, accompanied for an unknown time by its tail section, recommenced its slow, relentless movement south and east. As confirmation, the January 1942 photo shows the Electra past the bow and further south and east of the wreck by approximately ninety meters, and up-reef.

These are wonderful moments, and absolutely miraculous moments, inadvertently captured on film at key moments in the Electra's journey. But three photos are all that I have found. Four photos if you count the Bevington photo and the enhanced landing wheel. They're hardly a motion picture film yet they do tell an important story which is that the Electra made a journey of over 500 meters from the "Bevington object" or Electra landing wheel location found in Bevington's 1937 photograph, and at last (1942) glimpse, the Lockheed Electra wreckage was journeying on toward the mouth of the central lagoon.

The journey of the Electra along the reef edge took from sometime after July 2, possibly July 7, 1937 when radio signals from this area ceased, to June, 1941 and then January 1942 to be on the opposite side of the wreck from the landing wheel location in the 1937 Bevington photograph.

Where did the Electra go after January 1942? As far as I know, the next known photo of the shipwreck is a very blurred 1953 aerial photo which yielded nothing after I attempted to scrutinize it for detail.

Did the airplane wash into the depths? The Ballard search found nothing; no aluminum parts or pieces of an airplane were found. It is my belief that the reason why Robert Ballard found nothing in the ocean among the craggy cliffs off-reef, and the bottom, is because the bulk of the Electra is probably buried in the silt in the lagoon in the center of Nikumaroro. This makes sense if we believe natives who spoke of a wing and other aluminum airplane parts washing up on the lagoon beaches in later years.

The position of the Electra wreckage in the January 1942 photo may portend its ultimate destination of the lagoon's main channel several hundred meters away. But miracles do have their limits. We've no more photos to track the aircraft's progress with the tides. Also, remember that I've constructed an average movement. In large storms and large waves, the Electra may have moved significantly more than 46 cm on any given day, and vice-versa on calm days with no wind.

But let us not be ungrateful for the mere but fascinating three photos we do have and have added to the evidence that keeps unlocking parts of the mystery of the fates of Amelia Earhart and Fred Noonan.

For those of you who cannot understand or believe why no one noticed the Electra in this time period, 1937-1942, despite the island being visited and subsequently inhabited, I believe that no one went to the *Norwich City* shipwreck every day at low tide to look at it, let alone to take pictures of it. That part of the atoll was not popular, virtually uninhabited, and "taboo" to the villagers for various superstitious reasons, and the English overlords prohibited them from going there.

The village was across the lagoon entrance from the shipwreck and traversing the lagoon entrance on foot (swimming) was dangerous (sharks) and only possible at very limited time periods. Normally, such a journey required a boat ride to the other side of the lagoon (pulling on a rope strung across the lagoon), and then making for the beach and reef on foot to the shipwreck. Otherwise, one had to walk around the entire island or atoll, and then back—some ten miles.

The 1937/38 expedition and their photos seem to show a focus on the shipwreck and bow snapshots taken along with a huge piece of ship debris off the bow at the time. In fact, that large piece of wreckage can still be seen off the port bow of the shipwreck in the 1941 aerial photo.

None of these visitors or inhabitants were looking for an airplane or Earhart's Electra. I'm sure it was the farthest thing from their minds. Later, the knowledge that there was an airplane there on the reef became common knowledge, but the natives shunned the place. If the 1937 Bevington photo and the Electra landing wheel in it is to be believed, that wheel was over 500 meters west and north of the wreck. With the Electra submerged or hidden in deeper waters on the reef there in 1937 and throughout its journey along the reef in the surf, no wonder no one saw it except rarely.

Yes, I'm saying that for a ground observer to glimpse the Electra in the surf at Nikumaroro a hundred or hundreds of meters north and east of the wreck would have taken an even greater miracle of time, location, and sharp eyes because it was usually submerged or partially submerged.

Apparently, no one before me ever noticed what I saw captured in the instant the camera shutter was activated in these three aerial photos. You must also be aware of the mindset that debris in this area, even debris partially submerged, would impress the casual observer on the beach or reef there—as being debris from the shipwreck and not a submerged or partially submerged aircraft. And consequently, not worthy of a second glance or scrutiny.

Apparently, the aircraft (C-47) which took the January 1942 aerial photo was part of a relief effort dropping food to a beleaguered colony cutoff from resupply by the Second World War (1939-1945) and the Pacific theater that became a part of that war for the USA in the years (December 7) 1941-1945.

Did anyone in the village there on Nikumaroro take photographs? Or take photos germane to our search for

Earhart? Did any of the native settlers have a camera and film? Perhaps all answers should be "doubtful" or *No*. None exist. Expeditions there took photos in those early days, but *Norwich City* photos predominate and show the shipwreck and / or large chunks of the ship on the reef.

As I said earlier, the shipwreck itself is a huge distraction even to this day despite its near disappearance from corrosion after ninety years.

A similar experience comes from the natives on Hull Island who were contacted in July, 1937 by Lambrecht and the seaplanes from the *Colorado*. The people on Hull had never heard of Amelia Earhart let alone that she was missing. On the other hand, we, the searchers, are eagerly attuned to spotting the aircraft but no one was at the time these three photos of the *Norwich City* were taken.

Three or four "postcard" shots hid the answer all this time. And let's not forget that it's wet, with varying depths, on the reef according to the tide and the wind. And there are sharks, waves, and would you really wade into that surf, the tides turning, to look at huge, heavy and submerged objects, risking injury, possibly death?

No! It's just junk that has come off of the shipwreck. Let me take a shot of the bow!

I think you grasp my reasoning. Just remember that Amelia Earhart, day or night at low tide for one week, waded out to the Electra, climbed in, started the engine, and broadcast pleas for help. I'd like to believe that condensation inside her Electra on the windows and other surfaces might have provided some meager life-support to her during her struggle to survive.

From the progress made from the low tide-line or shallow water line by the Electra from June, 1941 to its position in January, 1942, starboard of the shipwrecked *Norwich City*, I will suggest to readers that within a few more months, perhaps a year, the Electra, just one more bunch of wreckage in a sea of wreckage from the ship, was washed into the nearby lagoon and disappeared under the silt and coral particles (see unenlarged 1942 photo presented in the beginning of the book for a viewpoint). Half of the tides per day take place in darkness or in partial or full moonlight, depending.

It is entirely possible that all the light aluminum wreckage is in the central lagoon, and that is the very reason why Robert Ballard found not one speck of aircraft aluminum during his intense and comprehensive search of the ocean and reef in August 2019. Of course, non-believers use this fact to totally discredit the Nikumaroro hypothesis. However, you can't say that conclusively without a complete and thorough survey and search of the lagoon. Remember, I've produced a pretty decent enlargement (plus two) of what most agree is an aircraft on the reef there 1938-1942 that looks a lot like the Electra in the factory photos presented herein.

As for the two massive and heavy P&W Wasp engines and landing gear wheels? I do not have an answer other than the native who claimed he salvaged a wasp engine from the reef and took it to another island. Like the landing wheel in the 1937 photo, they've vanished. Might the engine(s) still be attached in the photos I've displayed here? It's possible that one is and may account for them being no-shows on the ocean floor during Ballard's expedition because they or one of the engines and a crushed landing gear under the fuselage and wing stub are with the plane in the lagoon and covered in silt.

As for what happened to that landing wheel in the 1937 Bevington photo and its counterpart? Could it have moved more slowly than the Electra has been shown to be moving in the three photos due to its smaller surface area? Might it still be on the lip of the reef many hundreds of meters east and north of the shipwreck? Even west of it, somewhere?

I'd like to sit and watch all the drone footage shot by Ballard's team of the submerged reef area and the lagoon. I wonder if the wreckage of the landing gear and possibly one of the wasp engines still lie out there or in debris at the vegetation or "beach" line. TIGHAR documented coral berms from terrible storms on those beaches—what do they conceal?

During the National Geographic special, did you note that there was little or no footage of drone surveillance over the lagoon, or remote vehicles patrolling the lagoon for anomalies or what might be visible from the air?

What I saw on my TV screen were just a few postcard views or videos used as intros or transitions to the next scenes.

If Ballard could find one of the crew's hats on the bottom at 1,000 feet, then surely he would have spotted any aluminum Electra wreckage. I'm not trying to be funny. The absence of such wreckage and any aircraft aluminum find is an indicator that tends to support my theory that the Electra is in the lagoon though I'm perfectly willing to speculate that the Electra just continued its journey down the reef possibly all the way to the southern tip of the island. Then, speculate further that it started to go around the island to the opposite side? I think the lagoon is more likely.

At a rate of just 30-40 centimeters per day, two to three meters per week, 52 weeks per year, and 82 years on, assuming the aircraft stayed on the reef, this airplane may have traveled up to 11,000 meters or 11.25 kilometers. Nikumaroro is 7.5 km or 4.7 miles long. At that rate it had to have fallen off the reef at the extreme southern tip or may be lodged there somewhere below the surface at depth.

Could it be that whatever remains of the Electra aircraft is still on the reef and well to the south and east? I don't know. Something would have had to trap the Electra for some time to stop its steady progress but then the waves might have or would have battered it to pieces.

Yet, no aircraft aluminum was found by Robert Ballard. Ballard did say that if definitive proof of Amelia Earhart being on Nikumaroro is forthcoming, he will return to Nikumaroro and explore the beaches and area south and east of the *Norwich City*.

My hope is that Robert Ballard includes an extensive lagoon search as well.

Unfortunately, my discoveries in the photos displayed herein postdate his expedition by a few days. But what my discoveries and these photos reveal is that Earhart and Noonan did land there on Gardner on July 2, 1937 because there is the Electra on the reef and in the surf and moving along over the years south and east.

I'm hopeful that my work and discoveries reach Dr. Ballard's attention, and that a return visit will be made to Nikumaroro with more attention paid to the lagoon area and areas south on the reef. I did email these photos and an explanation to his email address at the University of Rhode Island and to his associate and director via their email. I do not know if he and/or she has seen the photos and narrative I sent because I have received no reply or acknowledgement, so far. I just hope that the men who absolutely feel they must control the narrative where Earhart is concerned, Ric Gillespie and Mike Campbell, and their collective snarls of "pareidolia illusion" and "fish-wrapper" are ignored.

These photos were my first series of two surprises in my work. I'm sure those of you who believe in the Saipan and Japanese prisoner scenarios feel that I've led you down the garden path using an engineered treatise hell-bent on supporting the TIGHAR position and everyone else who believes in it.

That was not my intention. I let the evidence speak for itself. Even a few military jockeys from our recent wars concur that that is an aircraft on the reef in those photos, and doesn't it closely resemble the factory pictures of a Lockheed 10E? All I've done is take evidence from July 6, 1937 and followed through along with revealing my discovery of the Electra image in the three photos taken of the *Norwich City* from 1938, June, 1941, and January, 1942, and the recently added January 30, 1939 photo taken of the Norwich City bow from the beach.

I believe this discovery of the Electra on the Nikumaroro or Gardner Island reef in the aerial photos puts to final rest any ideas that Earhart crash-landed in the ocean, on Saipan, or on New Guinea. Incidentally, a Japanese plane found there in New Guinea which closely resembled the Electra, which was originally thought to be Earhart's plane, was correctly identified thanks to an observation port in the nose which only the similarly constructed Japanese plane had.

Unlike others, I am unafraid of ridicule or disagreement. We lawyers thrive on it. I won all three of my immigration appeals in the Ninth Circuit Court of Appeals. Therefore, I invite anyone to refute my claims without resorting to simply shouting them down or dismissing them out of hand as illusions created by the brain. I've got three so-called "illusions" for you in these three photos, and my friend Patrick, the ex-US Army photo analyst, concurs that it's no illusion at all but an aluminum-like object with shadows and features consistent with the nose and fuselage of a Lockheed Electra.

How many Lockheed Electra aircraft went missing pre-January, 1942 in this area of the Pacific?

ONE! Amelia Earhart's Lockheed 10E Electra.

Ric Gillespie of TIGHAR chose to dismiss my evidence immediately without further analysis or study. My name isn't Glickman who is the person who drew Gillespie's attention to the "thing sticking out of the water" in the 1937 Bevington photo that led to the photo analysis and enhancement and the startling conclusion by experts that it was a landing wheel off the Electra. Gillespie missed that one but in fairness, he was looking at a cropped photo for quite some time.

Gillespie also didn't study the manual of the Norseman aircraft and failed to glean the presence of a type of parachute aboard the lost Glenn Miller plane to explain the "fisherman's" description of parachute cords or static lines streaming from an open passenger door. He missed that one, too. On May 12, 2020, in an article featuring TIGHAR's goal of raising $30,000 to study recovery of Glenn Miller's plane from the English Channel, Gillespie told a UK newspaper that TIGHAR had "researched" the issue of parachute static lines seen by the "fisherman" on the Norseman he had in his nets in 1985, and (TIGHAR) found the "parachute-equipped radio beacon" in the manual.

He's not telling the truth. I found that, not him or TIGHAR.

I recall at the time that Gillespie announced to members that my discovery of this feature of the Norseman aircraft in the manual was an example of "occult evidence."

He reminds me of the bombastic *Wizard of Oz*. So "occult" that he couldn't reveal the truth to the newspaper, or mention me or my name? Such is his control over everything TIGHAR, and Amelia Earhart, and his narratives thereon.

In hindsight, didn't anyone look at these photos of *Norwich City* for signs of the Electra or Electra-associated debris in the 30-year quest that TIGHAR has made for Earhart on Nikumaroro? In fairness, we all did and missed seeing the Electra. Some members of TIGHAR did state that they thought they had spotted Electra wreckage in photos but had not pressed the matter. I only saw the aircraft when I leaned back from my laptop and my eye went to the surf-line in the June 1941 photo and the Electra's nose just stared back from the photo. It was only upon enlarging the image that the true nature of what I was seeing was revealed.

At that moment, I recall saying, "You sneaky little bugger!"

Alright, I'll admit that my language was slightly more colorful.

I suppose that no other photo examiner or viewer ever saw this "hidden" image. I don't think they looked very hard. But yet, there is Ric Gillespie on the National Geographic special waxing profound on all things Amelia and stating that the Electra washed off the reef near where the landing wheel appears in the 1937 enhanced Eric Bevington photo.

Look, while I applaud the lengths and dedication that members of TIGHAR have gone to achieve the evidence they've found in three decades of searching, my view is they have not studied all the evidence or looked closely at these three photos presented, and others in their possession. Instead, my presentation and views were dismissed immediately and most responders in the forum sided with Gillespie's cries of "illusion" and his accompanying definition and description of how the brain connects random pieces of data to form faces and objects. Closing ranks, the core even remarked with words similar to, "Every newcomer tries to overturn thirty years of our study and discoveries."

Actually, this opposition encouraged me to press on.

Gillespie mentioned and alluded to "Raiders of the Lost Ark" during the National Geographic special and so will I. In the film, the Nazi's only have one side of the medallion, and their "staff of Ra" for use in the "map room" is too long. The line is, "They're digging in the wrong place!"

So too has Gillespie had Ballard searching in the wrong place because Gillespie sticks to original speculation and erroneously treats as fact that the Electra washed off the reef near the location of the enhanced landing wheel. It is still pure speculation today and now debunked by my photos that demonstrate the Electra plane that migrated along the reef for nearly 600 meters to the opposite side of the shipwreck by January 1942.

The same "illusion" and shadow configuration of Electra nose-hole and cockpit windows in three photos that span three years and three different locations? Let the professional photo analysts examine what I've found. I only knew one, my life-long friend Patrick S. of 55 years, who concurs in my analysis.

As for the assertion about the tail section? See for yourself in the following *composite* image which includes a shot of Earhart's Electra's tail section taken before this circumnavigation and tragedy. Personally, I think the tail is upside down because I think I discern the under-fuselage and protruding "bump" on top, the rudders possibly broken off, or submerged.

Ignore the circle in upper left which is ship debris I had circled by mistake. I've superimposed the January 1942 photo and you can see just above the fuselage a triangular, shiny shape. Then, above that is an actual photo of Earhart's Electra's tail section (ignore hat of bystander). Then, to the lower left right-angle of that photo, see also that triangular, shiny shape on the reef of the 1941 photo (the main photo above). I joined both with a thin blue line for you to compare them.

The following is a better shot of the Electra's tail section from a scale model of her plane:

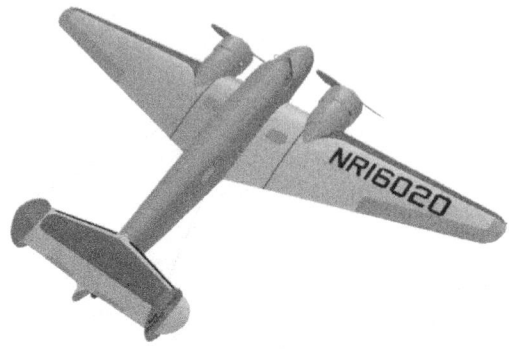

I think it is reasonable to conclude, in the absence of any further information or rebuttal, that that is actually the tail on the reef as well but minus the upright twin rudders (possibly upside down here) because it fits the shape, it's shiny, has the slanted leading edge, and it is certainly in proximity to the fuselage in the shallows.

Prior to my discoveries, there was one photo, an enlargement of the 1937 Bevington photo showing what is an Electra landing wheel upside down on the reef. To that single piece of evidence which Dr. Robert Ballard relied upon, I've added the fuselage of the Electra, possibly the tail section, and the fuselage visible in three photos: 1938, 1941, and 1942.

I will add one more photo for entertainment purposes, and not as further proof of the Electra's journey except to perhaps show consistency in my theory backed up by three wreckage photos. In prior editions, I mislabeled this photo as being from 1941. It is actually from 1942 when four PBY aircraft visited the atoll's inhabitants and shipwreck. I thought it might be the shadow of the Electra on the reef but a comparison with the silhouette of a PBY 5A says that I was incorrect, and Ric Gillespie was correct that one plane took an image as another plane passed by. The shadow is right there below a light gray image of the PBY fuselage. It may be on the following page.

 An aircraft has taken this shot south and east of the shipwreck. Near the center of the photo (mid-reef) is a dark shape that is remarkably like an aircraft silhouette. Keep this is mind. Look at the shipwreck. See the shadow and reflection of the ship in the water, including the mast reflection? That shadow is somewhat lengthy to the starboard of the shipwreck. Look at the bow of the ship. See how the reflection of the bow is nearly perfect, and only slightly forward of the actual bow? Nikumaroro is four degrees south of the Equator. The shadows here indicate the sun is low but possibly rising. You've seen your shadow lengthen as the sun sets. That shadow or plane silhouette is just a little too perfect. I believe this photo is explained as another aircraft passing through the camera view as the picture was taken.

The distinctive tail and silhouette of the PBY is evident. Look slightly left and behind this shadow silhouette of a plane, and what do you see? There is something light and shiny behind it. In fact, I make out the nose profile of an aircraft here just to the left and slightly beyond the "nose" of this dark shadow. I also see a line of white or light-colored metal across the top of the plane's silhouette shadow which is the sun reflecting off of a round surface. Then, look at the "tail" on this shadow. Isn't that a perfect shadow of an airplane rudder of the PBY? I added the below photos of the Electra here for comparison.

Definitely, the shadow of a PBY-5A and not the Lockheed Electra 10-E sitting on the beach which I had erroneously stated in an earlier edition. Interesting though is the telltale debris object that looks like a deer (vertical blue arrow) with tapered neck and ears just to the left of the sandy shoreline at the right side of that aerial photo. That debris was formerly just off the bow of the shipwreck in the earlier 1941 and 1942 photos (go back and take a look). Now, it is even closer to the lagoon's mouth by some 100 meters. I mention this to corroborate my statements that practically everything on this part of the reef winds up in or near the lagoon as the flow of the waves, water, is to the south and east most of the time. Which is why, because Ballard found no aluminum in the ocean, I believe the Electra wreckage is in the lagoon silt to this day.

This is consistent with the January 1942 image of the circled Electra found below (nose hatch hole, cockpit windows, etc.). See the deer-shaped object so close to the bow but so far away in the previous photo? The tail ends or wing-stub ends and the engine nacelles being the four small dots or reflections while the nose section reflects the most light and makes the larger white dot mentioned before and seen in the above photo.

As I often say herein, I wish I had more photos to analyze or more findings, but let's not be greedy, but instead be very grateful for what we do have. And can even my harshest critic admit that there is still data to be mined from these photos? Especially the original negatives sought since 1999 per TIGHAR with no update posted or follow-up?

Now, on to another aspect of this story. I'm not done, yet. I've one more surprise to bring to your attention in the next chapter which begins with one of the most bizarre reports in modern intelligence history which, if you believe in it, then you must believe that Amelia Earhart and Fred Noonan fell into the hands of the Japanese. As to how they did that at Gardner / Nikumaroro, an uninhabited island, I will also try to explain.

This next section of my book is my "fair play" and analysis of the Japanese capture theory. Mike Campbell of *Amelia Earhart, the Truth at Last*, a major proponent of the Japanese capture theory and Saipan, who dismissed my photo discoveries as *Take your fish wrapper somewhere else*, didn't bother to ask me how it might be possible for the Japanese to capture Earhart and Noonan despite the fact that Earhart and Noonan crash-landed on Gardner / Nikumaroro per my photo evidence of the Electra on that very reef.

Right, Campbell never listened nor afforded me the opportunity to explain how his book could easily piggyback on what I had discovered. It was silence and then outright hostility with no response allowed; Campbell said to his followers he had deliberately allowed me to post my photos so that he could slam me before his followers and thereby put to rest the hated "Nikumaroro Hypothesis."

The man detests Ric Gillespie with a passion. His anger and hostility have no place in science or in a free exchange of ideas and new discoveries.

Well, I'll stake my photo discoveries, especially the following photo from June of 1941, against his legions of "eyewitnesses" to Earhart's crash-landing any day!

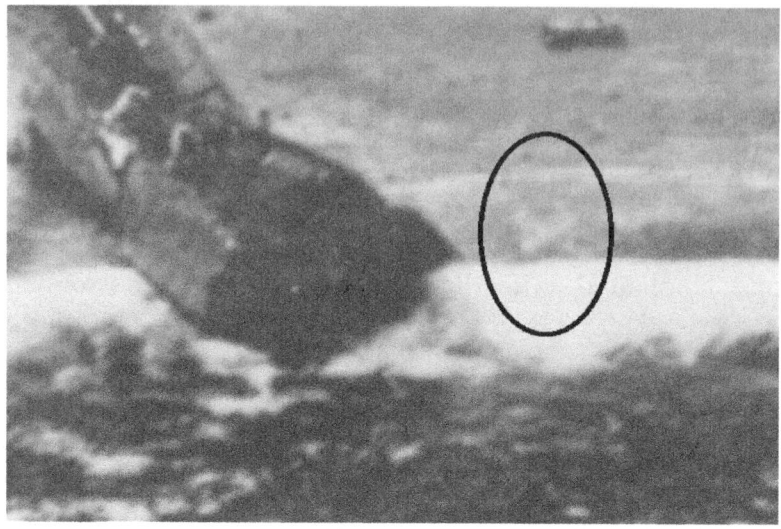

That's some fish! I'm taking the brunt of widespread criticism as well as frustration as my discoveries prove that these so-called historians and scientists failed miserably in their photographic homework. Or am I the only one who wonders if there is aircraft debris in other photos besides Cadet Bevington's postcard snap of the Norwich City magically enhanced into a landing wheel?

Why don't these other major Earhart punters assist in pursuing matters further? Such as put these photos or their originals to a full-forensic test?

I think we know why. Childish, isn't it?

It reminds me of Catholic clergy disdainfully dismissing the Protestant Bible by turning to the Lord's Prayer and reciting "...For thine is the kingdom..." in thundering tones and then accusingly saying, "How dare you have this heresy in your bookbag?"

"It's my grandmother's," I replied. My father's side was Church of England. There followed, slap, slap, slap.... *Those cruel bastards.*

7

Message in a Bottle

Perhaps some of you have seen this before or read about it. It's available at the National Archives on three pages and is old news, declassified in 1977 but "lost" until recently. I'll post the link because it is too difficult to place the pages here and fit it on the book page such that one can read it without magnification.

https://www.archives.gov/news/topics/earhart

Once you have this webpage up, <u>you will need to scroll down</u> to see all the documents discussed herein.

On this webpage has to be one of the strangest stories the intelligence services of the USA ever received: a French woman walking on the beach near the Gironde River and Bordeaux on October 30, 1938 spots a pint bottle sealed with wax in the sand. Inside are handwritten notes, a lock of light brown hair, and a chilling message. The woman turns the bottle over to the police who let the writer of this archived report view it before it was to be turned over to the US Embassy in Paris.

The writer of this archived report document which details what was in the sealed bottle is a US intelligence officer summoned by M. Hoppenot of the French Foreign Service Far Eastern Division in order to display the contents and to further show the American intelligence agent additional but similar information obtained from another French citizen.

The writer of the note in the bottle claims that he is dropping this bottle into the Mediterranean off the coast of Spain in the hopes it will drift to shore because he is in forced labor aboard a Japanese ship "Nippon Nom" (possibly Nippon Noru or Maru). He further states that his 25-ton yacht "VEVEO" was confiscated and sunk by the Japanese, his Maori crew of three killed, and he had been imprisoned in Jaluit prison in the Marshall Islands because he ventured too close to **Mila Atoll** and the large fortifications built by the Japanese there.

In other words, this man who penned this message in a bottle had been imprisoned as a spy. I could find no records of a yacht VEVEO. Alternatively, *Vevaios* means "of course" in Greek which is a not too surprising and appropriate name for a yacht. Perhaps VEVEO is just a mistaken phonetic spelling of *Vevaios* by a Frenchman who does not speak Greek?

The writer of this note in a bottle goes on to claim that he saw Amelia Earhart at Jaluit prison along with a man, a mechanic (Noonan presumably), as well as other European prisoners. The writer further states that this bottle is also a flotation device for another container containing things of Miss Earhart's. That container was never found. The writer claims the lock of brown hair in the bottle is from Earhart.

There is no record of what happened to that lock of hair or the fate of the bottle and its contents, whether it made it to the US Embassy in Paris or what they did with it if they had received it. As for our Embassy in Paris (later occupied France), Hitler did not declare war on the United States until December 10, 1941.

Anyway, it's useless to speculate about whether or not those artifacts reached the USA. They've never turned up or have been mentioned, again.

However, if this was a hoax (the bottle on the beach) then it was an overly elaborate one performed some fifteen months after Earhart is supposed to be lost at sea and dead. Can we give credence to this mystery message in a bottle? Or was it an elaborate, certainly over-the-top, hoax?

Now, if you are on the page of the US National Archives, keep reading and scrolling! This French official then shows the American an account of another French national; the tale of Eric Bissehop who sailed to Jaluit in early 1938. Upon arrival, Bissehop was cordially received by the Japanese until he mentioned that he had sailed past **Mila Atoll**, the same place the writer of the note in the mystery bottle attributed as the cause of his imprisonment. Then, Bissehop relates that Japanese cordiality instantly vanished, and he and his American wife were arrested, his yacht searched, until he was finally let go. The mention of Mila Atoll by both testators and their differing treatment by the Japanese does add some credence to the "message found in a bottle," and the Japanese reluctance to imprison an American (the Frenchman's wife) at this time of great secrecy during war preparation by the Japanese.

Then, at the bottom of the page the part about Earhart is torn! From studying it, the gist I get is that this man was asked about Earhart being a prisoner at Jaluit. Obviously, this statement was taken after the bottle was found on the beach unless the French Foreign Office had heard rumors about Earhart being a prisoner.

Apparently, Bissehop states "while possible..." and then mentions a man struck over... (the head?) on the same day he was there at Jaluit. What I find interesting between pages two and three is that they do not connect! Conspiracy alert?!

Page three starts a whole new narrative about the testator going on a yacht trip and to settle in Tahiti and how he had married his American wife in 1937.

Where is the continuation of page 2? Is it on the back? No. What it looks like to me is that the bottom of page three is taped on as a leaf across the bottom to conveniently display "page 3" at the bottom. There are missing pages from this report, one cries!

Hold on, it's easy to see conspiracy when there is none. To me, if the whole Earhart story as a Japanese prisoner is hogwash, then why go to such lengths to conceal this report or "major" parts of it? We'll never know, though it is suspicious, and woefully inadequate as a "fix" unworthy of a trained operative. After all, why not simply destroy the report? It would appear that in 1939, this report was altered by either the narrator or a superior or by order of a superior, or the letter was simply damaged during the 38 years it was in the hands of the archives. Where is that bottle and the hair sample?

I choose the latter explanation—the page was damaged.

I'm deliberately toying with you here. There's another, simpler explanation and that is that the torn off piece on page two has the short, missing part of the sentence from the same page: "...a spy" or "...executed" or perhaps, "...killed" and any number of possible combinations of two, three, or four words. He might have been a rapist, a saboteur, a smuggler, or anything.

I think you begin to see how easy it is to get on the conspiracy bandwagon. But I am intrigued by this Jaluit prison scenario and that Earhart and Noonan were reportedly seen there as prisoners as reported via the mysterious bottle message found on a French beach in late 1938, and many *eyewitnesses* per Mike Campbell's research in his book, *Amelia Earhart, The Truth at Last*. One Frenchman imprisoned performing forced servitude on a Japanese ship, but the other Frenchman let go because of his American wife? I see consistency in the differing Japanese treatment at the time if an American was involved in their suspicions. Japan did not wish to anger America at the time.

Did you see the Itasca radio log page on the same webpage and its (log) availability from the National Archives? Look at it for added perspective. Remember, it is the sanitized or finished log. Let's move on.

Recently, someone posted a photograph from the National Archives allegedly taken at Jaluit showing a group of people standing and sitting on a dock. In that photo, people identified Fred Noonan standing to the left of the photo near a "telephone" pole and a rear shot of a woman in profile, in short hair, resembling Amelia Earhart, sitting on the end of the dock.

Behind them in the photo is a Japanese vessel towing a barge with a seaplane, but viewers believed it was actually Earhart's Electra. The media went crazy about this photo and so did proponents of the scenario that Earhart was captured by the Japanese and that is her airplane being towed into the harbor while Earhart and Noonan hang about on a dock.

Not quite. See the photo below (or on the next page):

Below, or on the next page, is a captioned enlargement:

The History Channel took this photo and ran with it, and even had an expert agree that the pair resembled Earhart and Noonan. Then, reality struck. Military history buff Kota Yamano published a post showing the image in question contained in a book published in 1935—two years before Earhart even left on her round the world trip.

Oops! Everyone backtracked. Besides, where are the uniformed soldiers or guards? Security? And why would they allow anyone to take a photo that might reveal that the Japanese had captured Earhart and Noonan?

Now, it is easy to just say that the photo is meaningless, but I do believe *that is Fred Noonan* in that previous "dock" photo. Here, in the photo below, are Noonan and Earhart outside the Electra's cabin door. The hairline and shape with extended pointed hairline near his right eyebrow do seem consistent and visible in the Jaluit photo.

Humorously, with homage to *Occam* and his long beard if he never used his *razor* other than to make a point, then consider these facts: Noonan flew with Pan Am in those days. He was all over the Pacific in those "Clippers" and looking for landing places, additional and alternative destinations both for tourists, and for airplane refueling, maintenance, and emergencies in the early days of Pan Am.

Why couldn't he be here on this dock in that 1935 year—his image captured on film by a photographer for a travel magazine or publication?

Consider further that your author appears in the following: (1) The opening scenes of "Shaft", the original movie from 1969 with Richard Roundtree. I'm watching them film in Times Square with a friend. I'm in huge aviator sunglasses under a theater marquee while protestors circle in the foreground. I'm in another scene shot some thirty minutes later at the time but a few seconds after the previous shot on film. (2) I'm in the crowd during Mayor John Lindsay's NBC News interview in Union Square, Manhattan, on the first Earth Day held in April 1970. As the camera lifts on the crane at the conclusion of the interview, I'm there with those big aviator sunglasses. (3) I appeared on the cover of the souvenir booklet of Pompeii for some thirty years as a solitary figure in the middle of the Forum. Behind me is the photographer's wife under an archway who asked me to keep still (in 1976). I struck a pose, one foot forward and stared into the distance at her photographer husband on a higher platform, shooting down at us.

There are other instances of me appearing on the news and in newspapers throughout my life, and during my legal career. I think it is entirely possible that it is Fred Noonan in that photo on the dock. The resemblance is uncanny. Certainly, it is not unusual for an American to be there in 1935? And not unusual to resemble a man and have a similar hairline who flies for Pan Am in the Pacific, and appears in a photo of a known place in that Ocean during these "trips" he made in his career? This is the very reason Earhart or Mantz wanted him as a navigator on the round the world flight.

Consider this: What if that 1935 copyright of this travel publication does not reflect a later edition or subsequent printing? Say, one made in late 1937? I don't know. I raise this issue and my examples only to display for you my thinking and how and why one must ask questions and think critically without outright dismissal. There still may be key information lurking here that may cause a reassessment of this photo.

Is that Amelia Earhart? Unknown. If 1935, then no. If 1937, then yes because it might postdate July 2, 1937 and then, assuming that date, we know that somehow Noonan ended up here, and ergo, that must be Earhart. But again, *where* are the uniformed guards or soldiers for these so-called spies? I choose the 1935 explanation as the simplest explanation as *Occam's razor* commands. Still, no conclusion without further facts, but my comments do bear a closer look and investigation triggered by the very blogger (Kota Yamano) who countered the assertions of the History Channel.

The post by Kota Yamano interests me for the following reason which comes from his blog post:

"Palau: Futabaya Gofukuten, 1935, p. 44; from National Diet Library Digital Collection. According to original caption in Japanese, the photo taken at port of Jabor town in Jaluit Atoll. The steam ship on the right of the photo is a Japanese navy survey ship "*IJN Koshu.*" *The ship participated in searching mission for Amelia [Earhart] and arrived Jaluit Atoll in 1937*, but the ship also arrived there sometimes since 1935" (emphasis and italics are mine).

How interesting and how coincidental! The "fake" or misdated "Earhart" and Noonan photo features a Japanese Navy survey ship towing a seaplane that searched for Amelia Earhart some two years after the photo was allegedly taken and published in 1935.

Keep the IJN (Imperial Japanese Navy) *Koshu* in mind as we go forward, and that it had a *seaplane*. Also bear in mind that the Japanese stated that several of their warships participated in the search for Earhart and Noonan though latter-day researchers keep finding that those Japanese vessels were actually elsewhere or in port at the time (Japanese disinformation?). Japanese assistance in looking for the downed fliers is also mentioned in the US Navy reports filed after the search was called off.

Let me add one more item from that same page on the National Archives website which is also in the Putnam collection (see following page):

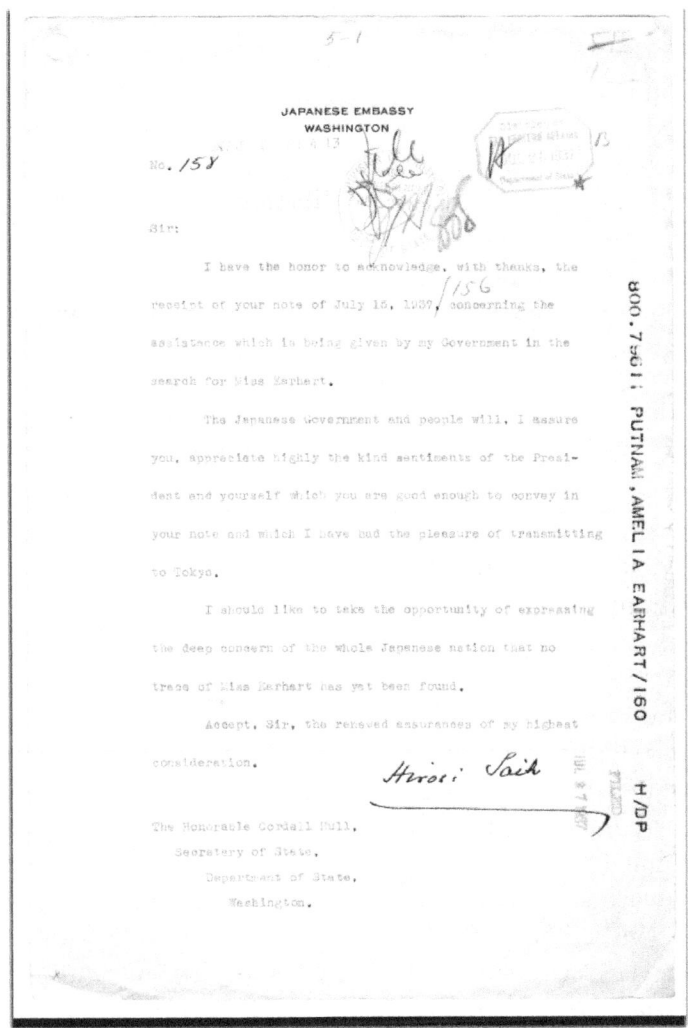

This letter addressed to Cordell Hull, Secretary of State, and received on July 20, 1937, is from Hirori Saito, Japanese Ambassador in Washington DC, expressing sympathy that no trace of Amelia Earhart had been found, and thanking the USA for their grateful note for the Japanese participation in said search for Earhart.

The US government called off the Earhart search on July 18. The letter mentions Hull's note of the 15th no doubt thanking the Japanese for their assistance. Recall that Japan had attacked China on July 9 just eleven days before, and that the US and Japan had exchanged "angry" words. That was the "same" day that the seaplanes from the *Colorado* buzzed Gardner Island looking for Earhart and Noonan.

Soon, FDR embargoes all sales of vital oil to Japan, precipitating war and the Japanese attack on Pearl Harbor on December 7, 1941.

In 1937, Japan was embarking on conquest and already had eyes on surrounding territories and islands, *and war*. The previous documents and statements from French citizens, reveal that Japan was dredging harbors for larger ships, making fortifications, bringing in guns and ammunition, and obviously preparing for war.

And the Japanese were paranoid about keeping such a build-up a secret from the United States. Perhaps this is the reason the Frenchman and his American wife were released unharmed with yacht and crew intact but not the other Frenchman who, while serving as a captured slave, threw that bizarre message in a bottle into the sea.

At that time, plans to build the giant mega-battleship *Yamato* were set for a keel laying commencing November 4, 1937 (in secret at docks near Hiroshima so as not to alarm the USA). The Yamato was completed in 1940 and did not participate effectively during the war but it had been planned for it to play a huge role. The mightiest battleship ever constructed was sunk by American torpedo planes and dive-bombers during what was termed a Japanese suicide mission to damage as much of the US fleet as it could near war's end.

Duplicity, secrecy, and a policy of expansionism tempered with a hatred of foreigners, particularly Whites and Europeans, represents the Japanese government's agenda and secrecy-paranoid atmosphere in 1937. Do you think that Hitler and Nazi Germany were the only believers in the concept of the master race? The Japanese believed in it and taught this concept to their people. For your information, modern China, the military government, also believes in this concept that they are the master race.

The two documents displayed by the French Foreign Service to an agent of US Intelligence are but a tiny example of Japanese brutality and their almost paranoid policy of secrecy at the time. This arrogance counted against them. The Japanese believed their codes were so superior (because of the belief *they* were superior) that no "White" man could break them. The USA broke all twelve major Japanese codes, and some were broken with help from Turing and other British codebreakers—a total of 25 codes in all were broken and gave away most of Japan's military secrets.

Such was the luck of the USA that in 1942, learning from decrypted Japanese codes that the Japanese were mounting another attack on the United States at "AF," the Navy and Naval Intelligence struggled to determine what "AF" referred to. The JN-25 code was a book or phrase code that was double and super-encrypted.

To discover what "AF" meant, a simple ruse was proposed because many thought the attack would be at Midway Island. To make sure, the island of Midway broadcast in the clear a simple noncoded lie that their water condensers had failed. Sure enough, the next day, an intercepted Japanese code decrypted to: "AF reports broken water condensers."

Because of this intelligence, just six months after the attack on Pearl Harbor, the USA was able to position its meager, remaining fleet off Midway to ambush the Japanese fleet. In that battle fought only by planes from carrier aircraft, in an amazing twenty minutes of the overall attack, the USA destroyed three Japanese aircraft carriers and later sank the fourth plus many other ships.

It was sweet revenge for what had occurred at Pearl Harbor against the very carriers and fliers who had participated in the sneak attack. From that June day in 1942, the Japanese tide was turned, and they went on the defensive for the rest of the war never able to recover from their loss of all those carriers, aircraft, pilots, and seamen.

In those days, Japan was a brutal regime, and I need not fill volumes with the atrocities they visited on just about everyone they considered an enemy. History books record that. However, I wanted to set the mood for you for our armchair rescue attempt of Amelia Earhart and Fred Noonan circa July 6, to July 9, 1937.

Newsflash: we're too late! Why?

I believe (speculate in order to link up theories) that sometime after July 7, 1937 when Earhart's last post-crash radio signal was heard in the early hours of the morning by a listener in Canada, and before the USS *Colorado*'s seaplanes arrived on July 9, a certain Japanese ship, the one in that Jaluit photo from 1935—*IJN Koshu*—which was participating in the search for Earhart, or another Japanese vessel showed up at Gardner Island / Nikumaroro and took the duo off the island. Or the widely reported "Japanese fishing boat" took them off the island and sailed them to eventual capture and internment in prison.

Japanese monitoring radios and direction-finders had stated (per US Navy report in National Archives) that the signals heard on Earhart's radio frequencies came from the Phoenix Islands. The *Koshu*, or other Japanese vessel listening to Earhart's broadcasts as Japanese civilians were also doing, and believing in their own people's superiority, had proceeded there to that location possibly listening for further broadcasts to perfect their navigational bearing and to locate Earhart. Their possible goal might have been to appear as heroes to the USA by rescuing Earhart and Noonan before the US military did.

Furthermore, Earhart had most likely taken her briefcase(s) from the doomed plane onto the island which contained her charts, maps, and other materials related to the flight, and the other briefcase containing all those commemorative envelopes picked up during the round-the-world trip. In our Japanese rescue scenario, the Japanese retrieved her briefcase(s) as well. Did the briefcase contain a letter from FDR or the US Navy to report on Japanese ships and assets as they flew over them? I can only imagine how horrific it must have been for Earhart and Noonan when they learned that their rescue and salvation was suddenly turned into forced imprisonment, and whatever horrors awaited them at the hands of their captors. I'm basing this speculation upon previous accounts of Japanese dealings with foreign spies.

Subsequently, the duo were allegedly executed on Saipan or elsewhere as spies based upon some compromising document in her briefcase, their flight route and the Japanese installations they flew over, and a court finding that they were spies, as attested to by people termed reliable eyewitnesses by other authors.

Yes, pure speculation on my part but a reasonable one designed to marry two competing theories as to the fate of Earhart and Noonan by simply connecting the dots and making logical inferences. In my book, I've proved Earhart crash-landed on Nikumaroro. I have nothing further to offer the other theorists except speculation, and the fact that I'm choosing to believe in the message in the mystery bottle found on a French beach on October 30, 1938 which I think is beyond being a hoax.

I'm basing my speculative scenario on the evidence of the Electra on the reef in the shipwreck photos, the evidence from July, 1937 that convincingly points to Gardner Island / Nikumaroro, and the statements in the documents the French Foreign Service showed to a US Intelligence official in 1939.

I will add to this the declaration of one Robert E. Wallack, a former US Marine who was 18 and stationed on Saipan after victory was declared over the Japanese.

Read his story for yourself here:
https://earharttruth.wordpress.com/2015/09/28/robert-wallacks-amazing-story-recounted-by-son-bill/

According to Wallack, he and his buddies with the help of a demolition guy blew open a safe they found in a government building while souvenir hunting on Saipan. Inside they found a briefcase (no signs of water damage Wallack said) and inside were the maps, passports, visas, and papers of Amelia Earhart.

Wallack claims he turned the briefcase and contents over to an officer with no insignia save for "scrambled eggs" on his hat, received a receipt for it, and never saw or heard about it again. Wallack was featured on NBC television with Connie Chung, and also on *Unsolved Mysteries* in Season three.

Wallack claimed that he was later wounded. And, in the medic's attempt to save his life, the carefully kept receipt for Earhart's briefcase was dislodged from his uniform and was lost. I also read this same explanation from another soldier who made similar claims about other "evidence" of Earhart.

There are similar stories by other soldiers of finding several boxes of Earhart's things found in caves on Saipan; another soldier's story featured discovering a room for a lady where a "10-year diary of Amelia Earhart" was found.

None of these items has ever turned up. The Smithsonian and National Archives chuckle about the many requests they get for these objects or pictures or documents concerning them. These requests are very easy for their respective agencies to handle—they have none and nothing, they say.

But several boxes of her things from an aircraft where she tried to save weight in Lae by lightening the load? I don't think so. The briefcase story I believe because it existed (there are photos of these briefcases, Earhart, and the Electra). The briefcase was important such that she would have taken it off a plane onto the island rather than let it be swept away with the Electra by the tides and waves.

The briefcases? There were two, actually. One was for all the stamped, cancelled, commemorative flight envelopes from around the world made during the flight supposedly to be auctioned off to help pay for the flight while the other briefcase held her maps, charts, passports, and other important papers.

I tend to believe Wallack and that he and his buddies found her briefcase. It is entirely possible that Japanese ships visited Gardner looking for Earhart but found only her briefcases and not her or Noonan's remains.

On Saipan, there existed Garapan prison where many believe Earhart and Noonan spent their last days before being executed. They must have been transported from Jaluit Atoll prison to Garapan prison on Saipan at some point. Perhaps to stand trial? The briefcase went along as evidence of her spying activities, I presume. Allegedly, Earhart and Noonan are both buried in an unmarked grave there on Saipan.

However, I'm not going to go into the minutiae of the Saipan scenario other than to say that I tend to believe in it but only to the extent that Earhart and Noonan ended up there as prisoners after being taken off Gardner Island by the Japanese Navy survey ship *Koshu* (or similar Japanese Naval vessel).

However, critically thinking, the briefcase may have been real, but does it follow that Earhart was found alive by the Japanese on Gardner? That Earhart accompanied that briefcase to prison? What about Noonan or just Noonan with Earhart dead? Or vice-versa? Noonan dead but Earhart still alive? We simply don't know.

Mike Campbell and his *Truth at Last* book also rely heavily on US soldier eyewitnesses who claim they burned Earhart's Electra found in a secret hangar; even swearing they saw NR16020 on the wings. Because I believe in the Electra wreckage images which I've found in aerial photos of Nikumaroro taken before WWII, I believe these soldiers saw a Japanese aircraft of similar design and elaborated and enhanced their tale with added detail. In fact, one such aircraft is only distinguishable from the American Lockheed by a window portal in an engine nacelle. No American soldier burned Earhart's aircraft. Nor, by any stretch of the imagination could the Japanese salvage the damaged aircraft off the reef at Gardner / Nikumaroro. One can hardly land a small boat there without using considerable skill. There is no landing place or blown-up section of the reef there at that time. And to land heavy equipment or to wrestle an artificially buoyed Electra in the surf and tide? Sorry, it's not feasible or possible in my view at Nikumaroro at the time (1937).

I also believe in the possibility that the *Koshu* or some other Japanese military vessel arrived at Gardner before July 9, 1937 (or even shortly afterward), the fliers were found dead, but the Japanese lifted the briefcase(s) and took both with them. There is evidence that the *Koshu* was refueling on July 13, 1937 on its way to the search and could not have reached Nikumaroro. In that case, I rely upon the mysterious "Japanese fishing boat" report that made the news which stated that Japanese fisherman without a radio had picked the fliers up. How they communicated that precise information to the media *without a radio* is another mystery, but it does smack of Japanese censorship or media manipulation. Perhaps they did have a radio. Perhaps it was a planted story to assuage the Japanese radio hams who were listening to Earhart's post-crash signals and desperate for news of her "rescue." These civilians all reported bearings that ended in the Phoenix islands or Kiribati as it is known today which includes Nikumaroro.

Naturally, the DNA tests now underway may identify that skull (it was only a cranium per Gallagher's notes) as belonging to Earhart, but it will be very difficult to prove the bones are the same ones found on Gardner Island in 1940 or that the skull came from Fiji after examination there. I don't think that the DNA test will confirm that it is Earhart. For one to believe in the scenario whereby Earhart and Noonan died at the hands of the Japanese as spies, one must believe that the skeletal remains found on Nikumaroro in 1940 were of some other person or persons unknown. Trouble is, no viable DNA has been found in that skull fragment. Three years later, there is no further news or progress on DNA.

But who or whom were those remains? We don't know. Did Noonan die and the Japanese left his remains there, but took Earhart? A shipwrecked yacht? A native couple shipwrecked on the island? A castaway that predated the wreck of the *Norwich City*? Anything is possible though there is no record of a shipwreck on Nikumaroro other than the *Norwich City*. What we do know or can surmise is that whomever it was had to have been dead before 1929 and the *Norwich City* wrecking on the reef, or thereafter, and before October 1937 when the island was visited by the expedition of which Cadet Eric Bevington was a part.

Admittedly, looking to all possibilities, it is entirely possible that Amelia Earhart and Fred Noonan did perish as castaways sometime between the final radio signals heard on July 7, 1937 and the arrival of the *Colorado's* seaplanes on July 9 even though a coconut jungle there on that part of the island where the shipwreck is might have sustained them for a few days if enough fresh coconuts had fallen to the ground. Can you envision an injured Noonan climbing a coconut tree? What about Earhart? Would there be enough "low-hanging" coconuts full of liquid?

As for skeletal remains found near the southern end of Gardner atoll, might the remains found in 1940 be those of Fred Noonan and/or Amelia Earhart, or even a mixture of her lower chest and torso but Noonan's skull fragment which threw off forensic analysis in Fiji? We don't know, and most likely never will.

The National Geographic special, "Expedition Amelia," which just aired (October 2019) confirms what I suspected; that the skull fragment was too degraded to get accurate base pairs. Apparently, forensic specialist Kimmele will have to try to find extractable, viable DNA for analysis. Note also that her own analysis of the pieced-together skull puts "European" as a low possibility. I think the bones found on Tarawa are a red herring and, unfortunately, a total bust. As stated, nothing further was developed by Kimmele.

My conclusions are these: What I've added to this story of Amelia Earhart is that the scenario of the Gardner Island / Nikumaroro emergency landing of the Electra is true, that the Electra is visible on the reef there in a 1938, (possible 1939), 1941, and a 1942 aerial photograph(s) of the shipwrecked *Norwich City*. Further, I believe that I have reasonably speculated that the Japanese assistance in the search for Earhart, and their listening to her in-flight and post-flight broadcasts plus their reading press reports at the time, led that Japanese Navy survey ship involved in the search, the IJN *Koshu* or its equivalent, right to Gardner Island where the Japanese "rescued" the duo on or about July 8, 1937 and subsequently transported them to Jaluit and imprisonment for espionage. From there, they were transported to Garapan prison on Saipan, tried, convicted of being spies, and executed.

Whether it was a Japanese navy ship or fishing boat as the vehicle that transported the fliers, the point is, with the Electra and Earhart and Noonan now on Gardner Island on July 2, 1937 per my photo discoveries, assuming the Japanese scenario of her fate is true, how else can I get Earhart and Noonan into the hands of the Japanese and off the island before the arrival of the searching seaplanes on July 9, 1937 unless I use the *Koshu* or another Japanese ship involved in searching for her to remove the fliers from the island?

That conclusion above (or finding them dead, the Japanese lifting the briefcases) is the only way this scenario could happen, and also explain the mystery bottle found on a French beach in 1938 which revealed an eyewitness account of seeing Earhart and her "mechanic" on Jaluit. I cannot prove it was not a hoax, but my speculative scenario certainly ties together the two leading theories about Earhart's disappearance.

I ask the obvious question: did *everyone* lie? That is as difficult to assume as the assumption that everyone is telling the truth.

All my logical inferences drawn herein stem from the photo discoveries I've made that the duo landed on Gardner / Nikumaroro which led to their ultimate fate at the hands of the Japanese Empire. That latter theory is advanced and believed in by so many including multiple "witnesses" to the fliers' presence on Saipan and before that on Jaluit Atoll. I chose to use the 1939 intelligence report about the mystery bottle found on the French beach in October 1938 because it is the earliest "evidence" we have that Earhart and Noonan may have been prisoners of the Japanese.

One scenario is now certain; Amelia Earhart and Fred Noonan were running low on fuel and Gardner Island or Nikumaroro is on that "line" which Amelia Earhart radioed as she flew back and forth in search of Howland Island. With no other place to land and not enough fuel to continue flying, Earhart landed on the reef at Gardner Island or Nikumaroro as it is presently known.

The photographic images I have discovered of the Electra on that reef are a monument to where her flight ended. No one else has discovered or put forth images of nearly her entire aircraft where many characteristic details of the Electra are visible. I'm forever grateful for the Lockheed factory photos made while Earhart's plane was repaired which reveal key features found in the presented aerial photos herein.

To those who assert that I rely too much on these aerial photographs, I remind them that I present a slew of circumstantial evidence in addition which has been built up over time by other researchers. The Bevington photo that shows the detached landing wheel of an Electra, the radio bearings on those post-crash signals all converging at Gardner Island, Betty Klenck's notes and the incredible accuracy of a minutes and seconds latitude position, the skeletal remains found in 1940 and Gallagher's report to his superiors that he believed the remains to be Earhart's (Earhardt's (sic) per report).

As to the fate of Earhart and Noonan after that landing, other than certain death by some means, and at some time, the mystery still exists and, absent hard proof, will remain speculation for some time to come.

I wish for you to imagine that *you are Amelia Earhart* coming in for a landing on that watery reef at Gardner Island on July 2, 1937 at approximately nine to ten o'clock in the morning local time. Your last _heard_ radio broadcast according to *Itasca* was "Wait..." at 8:44 a.m. You've been on edge having missed finding *Itasca* with a radio that doesn't appear to be receiving, and navigation that's off, way off.

I have no idea where we are. Fred says we're south of the Equator....

You're landing into the mid-morning Sun (assuming it was not cloudy). You've spotted a possible landing place while hopelessly lost in the vast Pacific. Howland Island is but a memory of a destination now that fuel is low. Survival is uppermost on your mind.

You have circled the island, viewing it from the air. It is a shape you have never seen before on any chart. The shipwreck there is still "fresh" after only eight years aground, but you have no idea what ship it is or when it ran aground the reef. It is a complete surprise. Perhaps, you or Fred will read the ship's name during a low-altitude flyby. The radio is useless; you can't raise anyone on any frequency. Perhaps no one heard you at all. The large, sufficiently wide reef area to the east and north of the wreck is your only hope for a landing. The reef is awash but looks to be quite shallow. You are lost, out of touch by radio, and low on fuel having dug into your reserve of 100 octane fuel in a last desperate attempt to find a landing spot. You've no choice but to accept this "gift" or a landing spot in the middle of nowhere.

You've flown over this part of the reef twice including a low altitude pass and have spotted nothing that might be an obstacle in your landing except for the shallow water and the massive ship aground on the reef.

You line up and begin your approach from the west of the ship. You will pass the bow on your port side and touch down hoping you can control the aircraft in this seemingly shallow water. You realize that the water might be inches or a few feet deep or both, possibly uneven below the surface. You toy with the idea of a wheels-up landing but decide to risk using the landing gear because you must turn an engine to power the radio. You're Amelia Earhart who has landed aircraft in farmers' fields and other marginal places. You've got this—you have to. There's no choice but to put down and soon.

You can't help but steal a quick glance as you pass the bow of the ship in your descent. Fred Noonan calls out the ship's name from the bow. You saw it, too. You tell Fred to watch the reef ahead and to prepare for a possible rough landing. You ease the plane down until you are just above the watery-reef surface. You flare and cut the engines back. The wheels hit the water and the props whip up spray from the water. The slight cant or angle of the reef finds your starboard wheel hitting the water surface first. You settle the aircraft but resistance on one side of the plane forces you to over-correct to the other side. It's the Hawaii ground-loop accident all over again. The landing gear collapses, and the plane turns and spins toward the ocean. A wing breaks. Debris from the reef batters your cockpit windows while the sudden lurching causes Noonan to hit his head, injuring him. The plane comes to rest.

You and Fred Noonan are alive! Quickly you glance out your window at the surf and the shallow water that surrounds you. You ignore Fred's complaints of injury. Then, one engine useless with propeller bent, you unstrap and hastily open the upper cockpit hatch and look over your plane by leaning out. What you see is hopeless. The plane is immovable from this spot with one collapsed landing gear, and a broken or bent wing. The engine that powers the radio is undamaged, and you've left it idling just in case this is your only opportunity to send a *mayday*.

You realize the tide will rise because you see the high-tide mark clearly on the large ship's hull behind you. You also realize that the Electra's propeller must clear the water. You duck back inside the aircraft to view Fred who is in a bad state, possibly injured. Water is rising! Fred Noonan is panicking, calling out to his wife Mary Bea. Your glance takes in the port cabin door and that the bottom of it is obviously underwater. You can't afford to open that cabin door without risking flooding the cabin. You'll have to climb in and out through the cockpit access hatch forward of the wing.

It's getting very hot inside the plane even though you've left the cockpit access window open.

"I'm going to radio that we're down on an island," you quickly say to calm Fred Noonan.

Your heart bursts with relief that the engine still functions and that the propeller blades are clear of the water. You switch to the daytime frequency, 6210, and key the microphone but Fred distracts you with calls or cries to his wife "Mary Bea."

"Will you help me?" you softly ask when Fred has a moment of calm (Betty's notes).

Grumbling, Noonan agrees. You begin to broadcast while unaware that perhaps only a 15-year-old high school girl in Florida will hear you and write down part of what you say, and only what she can hear and understand, intermittently. Naturally, your first message on July 2, 1937 is lengthy. Fred Noonan is with you in the cockpit because you have not yet left the aircraft for the first time. And for all you know, this may be the _only_ possibility to radio for help should the unknown, upcoming tidal depth and the waves take the aircraft out to sea!

"This is KHAQQ. We have landed on a small island reef some 200 miles south of Howland. There is a shipwreck here. The _Norwich City_...."

Unbeknownst to you, only fragments of your message are heard. Some hear you saying your name. Betty Klenck hears you say the name of the ship but thinks you say _New York City_, and she hears you and Fred Noonan converse and argue. Two days from now as you repeat this information, a boy of sixteen will hear you in Wyoming and hear a little more detail than Betty does today. You look at your navigator. Noonan is frightened, injured, raising his voice, but you keep broadcasting because you know that the tide is rising, and this may be your only chance to broadcast your whereabouts. Obviously, you also keep the transmit button depressed as you try to calm Fred Noonan.

The rising water on the reef spooks Fred. You give thoughts to abandoning the plane, going ashore toward the narrow beach and scrub while carrying your important papers in your briefcase(s) along with whatever you can salvage from the aircraft that will be useful. You give thoughts to water and food of which you have little thanks to weight-saving measures you took in Lae, New Guinea. Maybe a few cans of your favorite tomato juice are still left in the cockpit? After you shut down the engine, you look for them. The envelopes and stamps in one briefcase seem useless now and you dump them out into the cabin to make room for any liquids and food you might have including any useful tools.

Perhaps you will find water and food ashore? As the rising water, tide, and approaching surf line compel you to abandon the aircraft, you and Fred gather what essentials you can and carry them toward the narrow strip of beach. Fred takes his sextants but makes you carry one because he is unsure that he won't fall as he exits the aircraft and wades through the rising water. Depositing Noonan on the beach or shingle, you make several trips to the Electra to carry ashore what you think will assist you.

You'll need shelter from the sun. You also want to keep an eye on the plane. So, you ferry yourselves and your meager provisions to shore directly opposite the Electra. There, you will try to find shelter and a line of sight to the plane. This effort taxes you both. You drink from a can or bottle of tomato juice. You make Fred comfortable and then return to the plane for more necessities. Meanwhile, you fervently hope that the next low tide will allow you to broadcast again.

Your thoughts turn to fire, shelter, food, and <u>water</u>. Perhaps, you also think of an emergency signal? A large fire to attract passing ships. You're exhausted but alive. You don't expect airplanes out here so you dismiss any effort to write a message in the coral sand or scrub.

As you perspire freely in the heat and humidity, your clothing is soaked with sweat as well as brine from wading on the reef. Upon returning to Fred under a tree near the shoreline, you catch sight of two large coconut crabs at the narrow strip of dry beach near some scrub. You wonder if they have come to wait for a very large meal. You shake your head to be rid of this horrible image. You proceed to drape your head and Noonan's in cloth to protect your heads from the sun. This shade and shelter will do for now as the sun moves southward but higher in the sky.

Eventually, you will seek better shelter for the night, and a place to build a fire. You reconnoiter the large group of trees but find that you cannot see the beach or the Electra. You find some coconuts and shake them. You hear liquid inside. Your small knife seems inadequate for the task because you don't know how to husk a coconut using a sharpened stick. Here, Fred comes in handy because he knows the trick having seen natives in the Pacific perform it. The fire lit, your clothing is salt-encrusted, rough, and uncomfortable. You rest for a while in your underwear, and Fred does the same.

Soon, you'll be up and looking for water and thinking about what you can eat. It's summer and daylight lingers. The lagoon offers turtles and fish if you can catch them, and if you can find a way through the thick undergrowth to get to the lagoon. You try walking to the lagoon entrance first and walk to it via the thin shoreline beach. Fred suggests that throwing a coconut crab on a fire will allow you to eat. This meal and others you scrounge later, help you survive a little longer.

Little do you realize that, despite surviving this leg of the journey and landing fairly safely, you are doomed by the same mistakes that forced you to land here. It's one of the driest seasons in this part of the Pacific. You look skyward and to the visible horizons. You don't know that there is no fresh water here.

It had better rain, and soon," Fred says, nursing his head injury. "I'll walk north and east and take a sun shot and give you our position. That ought to help."

"What island is this do you think?" you query.

"Damned if I know. Hopefully, that shipwreck name will guide them to us. If we don't find water soon, we can't last but a few days even if we eat a lot of crab and fish. There may be a lot of coconuts here judging by those many palms. They must be very old to be so tall. Good luck climbing any of them. We're limited to the ground and maybe a lucky throw with a hunk of coral. That might give us a few days more."

"I'll gather whatever is dry for the fire. Keep an eye on the plane. And listen for anyone who might live here."

"Saw no one from the air, Amelia. It's just us."

"I hope they heard me."

"Nobody heard you all the way here!"

"Fred? Let's try to survive as long as we can. Get me that position and I'll broadcast again before the tide is too high. Then, in about twelve hours I'll broadcast at the next low tide."

"I can see the plane moving in the water from here. In a few days, the sea will take her…. Damn, what a mess."

"Your lighter will come in handy. Have a cigarette, Fred."

"Yeah. I think we're further south. Possibly 300 miles from Howland. I'll let you know our position. Give me a sip of your drink, and I'll work on that fix so you can radio our position…."

For six days, you run out to the airplane twice a day, including nights, at low tide to fire up the engine to allow you to broadcast. Then, on July 7, you run out of fuel. Over the past several days, several faint messages were heard by you, and you broadcast the three tones and the requested letters every time but, other than hope, no help is forthcoming....

You are both doomed.

8

Japanese Codebreakers: The Price

Were you aware that the chief architect of the system to crack the JN-25 Japanese Naval code was a woman? Agnes Meyer Driscoll, fluent in Japanese, served until 1949 and was considered one of the top cryptanalysts of her time.

Then, there wasn't just one Japanese code. There were many: twelve main ones and many diplomatic, merchant, and other codes. Due to the codebreaking by US Naval Intelligence, the USA knew Japan's limits on negotiations for the size of their naval fleet. At the League of Nations, Japan settled for a fleet half the size they desired as the USA and Britain negotiated accordingly.

Japan subsequently quit the League of Nations exposing it for the impotent organization that it was. The Japanese began building their naval fleet and arming in secret, preparing for conquest and war. The *Yamato* keel was laid in November 1937. Plans for that battleship, the biggest ever built, must have been made long before Earhart's flight.

Commencing in the 1920's, after the US Government reconsidered its appalling anti-espionage mantra that it was "ungentlemanly to read another's private correspondence," the United States revamped their cryptography groups and was reading many of the Japanese "book" codes on the diplomatic and merchant levels with significant inroads made in other codes. I've little doubt that somewhere in US intelligence a Japanese coded message revealed or partially revealed that the Japanese had both Amelia Earhart and Fred Noonan as prisoners, or that they had found them dead.

This is pure speculation on my part but if my scenario of the flyers being taken from Gardner Island by the *Koshu* or other Japanese military search vessel is correct, sooner or later, the codes the Japanese thought were invincible would give up the secret to the US codebreakers that the Japanese had captured as spies both Earhart and Noonan.

Now, what would US Intelligence or the US government do about such a revelation? They kept it a secret, I believe. They had to. But secret until 2022? Even the Germans and the saga of cracking their Enigma codes is fodder for books and movies. This is one of the reasons why I don't believe Earhart and Noonan were prisoners of the Japanese. However, let's give the scenario fair play.

In Fred Goerner's 1966 bestseller, **The Search for Amelia Earhart,** the author recalled his first meeting with Commander John Pillsbury, public information officer for the 12th Naval District, in connection with Goerner's work on a 1962 radio documentary *The Silent Thunder*.

Therein, the author was told via Pillsbury that "Admiral Nimitz wants you to continue and you're on to something that will stagger your imagination."

See:

https://earharttruth.wordpress.com/tag/admiral-chester-w-nimitz/

In the book, *Truth at Last*, Campbell twists this statement into support for finding the wreckage of Earhart's plane in the jungle on Rabaul, New Britain Island because that author believes Earhart turned back toward the Gilberts when she couldn't find Howland Island. As I have also done, that author relies on Robert Wallack finding Earhart's briefcase on Saipan in a blown-open safe, and a series of "witnesses," plus his own analysis.

Nimitz is not quoted as saying that the Japanese had Earhart and Noonan, it is inferred by the author instead. In view of my finding images of the Electra which proves Earhart did land on Gardner Island, only the scenario that

Earhart and Noonan wound up as prisoners of the Japanese remains to be verified. I added my own speculation to this scenario by suggesting the Japanese Navy did rescue the fliers but imprisoned them for espionage because of compromising papers found in Earhart's briefcase.

Whether the statement attributed to Nimitz is true and inferences drawn from that are also true and correct, or not, one can see how our government, if they asked the Japanese to return Earhart and Noonan to the USA, would compromise security and reveal to the Japanese that we had broken their codes.

Code breaking was a major contributor to winning the war against the Japanese, and perhaps Amelia Earhart and Fred Noonan had to be sacrificed for the proverbial "greater good."

Even if the statement attributable to Nimitz is false, it doesn't remove the need for keeping secret our codebreaking accomplishments and, Nimitz or no Nimitz, we could not ask Japan to return Earhart and Noonan without begging the question, how could we know?

In any event, the evidence and proof I've put forth that the Electra was on the reef at Gardner Island on July 2, 1937 (and never took off again) effectively quashes any of these authors' scenarios that she crashed-landed elsewhere.

How about using the message in the bottle found near Bordeaux as proof of how the "American government" learned that Earhart and Noonan were prisoners of the Japanese? That assertion would have been met with polite Japanese laughter, and a stoic denial. Then what?

Sometimes, knowing a secret ends up compromising the thinking of the holder of that secret. For example, Prime Minister Winston Churchill of England knew of the pending air-attack by the Nazis on Coventry but did not warn the populace because he didn't dare compromise *Ultra* or that Bletchley Park had broken Germany's *Enigma* codes. The center of Coventry was destroyed, and 451 lives were lost and over 700 were wounded. But the secret of *Ultra* was kept.

In the case of the Battle of Midway, scouting aircraft were sent out to find the Japanese fleet, *and* to be seen by them. This was deliberate and necessary so that attacking torpedo planes and dive bombers could navigate to and destroy the Japanese fleet. The US scout planes were spotted and fired upon and provided the excuse that we learned of the Japanese attack on Midway by means other than breaking their codes.

Indeed, Winston Churchill mandated that no secret gleaned from breaking Nazi codes could be acted upon unless another independent means was handy and could be used to explain away Allied actions.

Later in the war, intercepted and decoded Japanese messages gave the USA Admiral Yamamoto's itinerary. A waiting squadron of P-38 Lightning fighters ambushed him and shot his plane down. Yamamoto's death was a huge blow to the Japanese who thought their hero had succumbed to the bad luck of encountering a routine American patrol.

Earhart and Noonan could not have picked a worse time to try to traverse the Pacific. Rumors abounded that FDR had some secret mission or task for Earhart as she flew. Perhaps, in her briefcase, were instructions outlining the plan or surveillance. Logically, Earhart either had forgotten about them or was surprised on Gardner Island by Japanese sailors, captured along with her briefcase, and before she could rid her briefcase of compromising materials. Again, pure speculation on my part but reasonable if you support my version of things after July 7, 1937 when her radio signals ceased and why the duo did not wave to the seaplanes from the beaches of Gardner Island (unless they were dead) on July 9.

If you agree with me that Earhart's Electra is on the reef in any of those three photos, The *Koshu* rescue scenario I'm advancing helps explain why no one found her or Noonan there (or until bones were discovered two years after habitation of Gardner Island recommenced in 1938). And it explains why, within two days of her last broadcast, no one greeted the US Navy planes that buzzed the island. Unfortunately, the Japanese were looking for her and the *Koshu* (or similar Japanese ship) found her first. Imagine the seaplane of that Japanese ship landing in the lagoon? That seaplane solves the problem of landing a small boat on that treacherous reef in 1937.

Then, it is entirely possible that indeed Earhart and Noonan perished from thirst as castaways on Gardner / Nikumaroro. Consider that the Japanese did land there in the *Koshu* or some other ship before July 9, 1937 but found the two flyers dead. They took her briefcase, examined it, and perhaps other personal effects. They found evidence she was a spy, at least by their standard. They returned to the ship with the briefcase, sailed away, and kept silent about their discovery.

But the message in the bottle found in France in 1938, the possible existence of, and unknown contents, of top-secret decryptions of Japanese coded messages, and other "evidence" is counter to my speculation. I merely place this possible scenario here for your interest and as evidence of my thinking of all possibilities. I will not speculate unnecessarily about what happened between Noonan and Earhart as thirst drove them into madness and desperation. A horrible possibility but both possible and probable.

Note that any solid piece of evidence unearthed in future that places the flyers elsewhere will clinch this double scenario that I have carefully presented now that there should be no doubt Earhart crash-landed on Nikumaroro or Gardner Island on July 2, 1937 and did not take off again in the Electra.

Will we ever know the whole truth? Even a hundred years on, in 2037, I doubt the US Government would be willing to admit that they willingly abandoned "Lady Lindy," the beloved heroine of the American people and one of the most famous and admired American women in history, to the Japanese without a fight or concerted effort to save her.

Codes or no codes, the backlash would be severe in my opinion. In the former political clime, under the Trump administration, abandonment (of allies and principles) is a hot issue. I believe that revealing today that FDR knew Earhart was a prisoner of the Japanese would forever tarnish his reputation and the reputation of the USA.

Unless uncovered by others, the truth will not be forthcoming from the government if the US knew of her capture and imprisonment back in 1937-1939. From the stories told by soldiers of having discovered Earhart's personal belongings, particularly Wallack finding her briefcase and passport within a safe on Saipan, and the subsequent silence that ensued along with the disappearance of those belongings, I infer that even though the war was won, the government could not afford this secret to be revealed.

Ask yourselves, as armchair intelligence officers, would you reveal that you knew this information as far back as 1937, and that you or your government did nothing? I can understand why from an intelligence viewpoint during the war and further understand the international and national embarrassment after the war should such information be made public. Especially the backlash all interned Japanese Americans might face when they were freed and allowed to return to society.

However, though I understand the motives, I would have come clean about it by now. Usually, seventy years is the benchmark for declassification of secret information. We've revealed to the world that we had broken the Japanese codes as well as the Nazi *Enigma* codes and other secrets. So, why not reveal the truth about Earhart and Noonan being Japanese prisoners?

Two possibilities: either I and other proponents of this scenario are wrong or that everyone either made up or were mistaken that Earhart was a prisoner of the Japanese. Otherwise, the truth of her capture and execution, if it exists, must be extremely embarrassing and must be kept secret to this day and for the foreseeable future.

Regardless, they perished sometime, somewhere, after landing on Nikumaroro / Gardner, victims of their own folly in failing to establish effective radio communication protocols with *Itasca* before they took off from Lae in New Guinea.

9

Conclusion

This narrative has had three purposes: the first was to bolster and support the scenario whereby Amelia Earhart and Fred Noonan did in fact land on Gardner Island (Nikumaroro) on July 2, 1937; the second purpose was to offer an alternate and plausible explanation of what happened to the two fliers after said date; and thirdly, to join two competing scenarios into one.

For the Gardner Island landing, I have presented the usual facts many have used to support this scenario including the radio signals, bearings made from radio direction-finders, and the purported content of Earhart's alleged radio signals.

Additionally, I have presented three (and a newly added fourth) aerial photos of the *Norwich City* shipwreck taken in 1938, (1939), 1941 and 1942 that reveal the Lockheed Electra on the reef near the surf line port of the wreck in December 1938 and by (1939) 1941 the Electra wreckage is to the starboard of the wreck, and off the starboard bow of the wreck in the January, 1942 photo. The latter two photos show at least the nose section to just behind what remains of the wings of Earhart's Electra.

There is a possibility that comprehensive photo analysis might also identify the tail section which I report seeing in both latter photos; the 1942 photo possibly showing the tail section broken off and oriented 180 degrees behind the nose/cockpit image.

From this photo evidence which I've discovered plus the image of the Electra's landing wheel in the Bevington photo of 1937, I conclude that Earhart did not crash into the ocean or on Saipan. She crash-landed on Gardner Island and did not take off from that island *in the Electra*.

From the many post-crash radio signals picked up by amateurs and professionals along with bearings on said signals given by the professional and military radio operators, I conclude that these bearings which intersect near or on Gardner Island (Nikumaroro) plus the images of the Electra I've found, conclusively add to the proof that Amelia Earhart crash-landed there.

Once one believes (as Robert Ballard does) or is convinced of the authenticity of just one of those post-crash signals and its Nikumaroro or Gardner Island bearing, the information reported as to what was said by either Earhart or Noonan in said broadcasts further lends credence to landing on this atoll. The broadcasts report that Earhart is on a reef, an uninhabited island south of the Equator, possibly a shipwreck on the reef, that water is rising rapidly around the Electra due to the tide, and that she and Noonan cannot last much longer.

Accepting the radio broadcasts requires that the Electra must be on land in order for the engine to run to charge the batteries and power the radio. From the descriptions from various broadcasts, the Electra was on a reef vulnerable to rising tides which means that the engine could only be run as long as the propeller cleared the level of the tide.

These same broadcasts contain clues that the aircraft was not stable on the reef, and it is reasonable to assume that the Electra was pulled further out to sea until it was submerged beyond an ability to run the engine but was still on the reef. The last signal came early on the morning of July 7, 1937 and no further broadcasts were heard, apparently, save one reported on July 8 but very fragmentary, and quite possibly accomplished from scrounged fuel from the bottom of near-empty fuel tanks or the other engine in a true, final effort to be heard and rescued.

The Eric Bevington photo circa October 1937, taken some three months after the Earhart disappearance and crash-landing, prompted Robert Ballard to explore the reef of Nikumaroro after it was revealed that experts in photo analysis and enhancement concluded that the small image on said photo is the landing wheel of an Electra sticking up on the reef in shallow water.

My eyes easily pick out the "Y" shaped yoke around the wheel in the Bevington photo as well as the gearing for extending and retracting the landing wheel. I agree that the enhanced photo is that of an Electra landing gear.

If one believes in the landing wheel some 500 meters north and west of the shipwreck *Norwich City*, then one must also believe that the rest of the aircraft has to be somewhere on or near Gardner / Nikumaroro. My conclusion from seeing the Electra nose section and wings *on the other side* (SE) of the Norwich City in a June 1941 photo, and in a January, 1942 photo, leads me to conclude that the Electra, submerged but still on the reef, slowly made its way southward and eastward toward the shipwreck through tidal and wave action, passed the bow, and then washed down to the shallows at low tide just starboard of the stern in the lee afforded by the shipwreck. This progress is confirmed by the 1938 photo of the *Norwich City* which shows the Electra aircraft still some 150 meters from the *port* side of the shipwreck. Then, the new photo I found from January 30, 1939 confirms the Electra, or perhaps only the tail boom and fuselage up to the trailing edges of the wings, has transited to the starboard side of the shipwreck by at least that date.

From the calculated position of the Electra landing wheel in the 1937 photo, that is a distance of approximately 500 meters and a possible journey for the Electra (given the earlier date of 1/30/39) over a time period of approximately 19 months (or 44-47 months for a June, 1941 date) to get from a position on the reef at the Bevington landing wheel location all the way past the shipwreck, then down to the low-tide surf-line, and thence to a position higher on the reef and further east and south in the January, 1942 photo.

Because of this earlier photograph I discovered, and assuming that I'm correct that the wreckage seen in the water is the Electra, then the Electra moved at the rate of approximately 46/100 of a meter per day south and east to reach and then go around the bow of the *Norwich City*.

The debris flow evident in the photos presented and many other photos of the wreck and its debris do show a steady migration of wreckage from the shipwreck in the general directions of east and south to the mouth of the lagoon.

The "longshore flow" at this part of the island is such that the heavy Electra fuselage remnant moved slowly day by day, relentlessly south and east, possibly washing up higher then lower on the reef in repeated cycles per the two high tides and two low tides that occurred during every 24 hours and fifty minutes.

If the evidence in the 1/30/1939 photo of the ship and possible Electra tail-boom wreckage to starboard thereof is too tenuous, then to achieve that same position as clearly visible and obvious from the June, 1941 photo of the Electra in the surf line, then a time period of forty-seven months, or 1,430 days approximately, and assuming an average for daily movement, the Electra fuselage only needed to move approximately sixteen inches or 35 centimeters per day during the daily, double high and low tides in order to traverse 500 meters during that time period. Perhaps 18 inches and 46 centimeters average per day for the Electra to be on the starboard side of the shipwreck. This is an average calculation and does not take into account storms, high-wind-driven waves. or "super" tides. On a per-tide cycle of a single low and a single high tide, the water and wave action need only move the Electra approximately nine inches or 22 centimeters.

Not unreasonable at all. Note that most debris on the reef follows this wave and tidally driven path toward the lagoon and the opposite side of the lagoon entrance.

These movements are reasonable. In fact, given the length of the shipwreck, or what's left of it in the 1941 photo (stern broke off in 1938), and the Electra debris position six months later in the January 1942 photo, just seven months in the lee of the shipwreck managed to push the Electra from the low-tide surf-line up onto the reef to appear past and to the south and east of the bow of the shipwreck, and headed in the direction of the main lagoon channel several hundred meters distant—accompanied by a lot of ship's debris.

How many times had the Electra cycled back and forth due to the tides in that time period? About 2,900 times. How long was it on the opposite side (starboard) of the shipwrecked *Norwich City* post June 1941? I don't know. I'm unable to calculate exactly what distance this is between the 1941 and 1942 positions in the photos, but, based upon the length of the wreck next to it, it is at least 200 feet or near 75 meters.

Using our average movement calculation for four tides per day, 180-210 days (between 1941 and 1942 photos) times 18 inches or 46 centimeters would be approximately 240 feet to 315 feet, or approximately 72 meters to 100 meters.

This seems to fit the average drift calculation quite well and the approximate positions of the wreckage in the two aerial photos from 1941 and 1942 as measured by what remains of the length of the hull of the shipwreck. It doesn't fit when one considers the 1/30/39 photo and possible Electra fuselage in the water starboard of the ship unless one speeds up the average daily Electra movement via the tides by increasing it. And even that distance per day is not incredible and still quite plausible.

However, the Electra is then in the shipwreck's lee (on the starboard side) as to the drift and flow of the waves and water on the reef which I believe accounts for its slower progress up the reef at this point as far as its distance southeast from the bow of the shipwreck in the 1942 photo seven months later. Perhaps Winter and associated storms provided enough force to move the Electra wreckage out of the lee of the *Norwich City* shipwreck.

This movement up the reef may support my speculation that the Electra was slated to be washed into the lagoon channel and thence into the silty, and coral rubble-filled lagoon. From January 1942, I can only speculate and rely upon reports that natives living on Nikumaroro from 1938-1963 stated that airplane parts washed up in the lagoon from time to time, including a "wing" from which they used the metal to forge implements. One native said that the aircraft itself was sometimes visible at low tide but the shipwreck obscured observation from the village locale on the other side of the lagoon channel from the shipwreck.

Bear in mind that the British authority there put the area around the *Norwich City* off limits after they collected bones of the (presumed) disinterred three bodies of drowned Norwich City crew which the captain dutifully reported he and survivors had buried opposite the bow of the aground ship.

I believe that my discoveries in those aerial photos, substantiate the truth of the anecdotal information derived from natives who lived there at the time of finding airplane debris.

Judging from the general direction of the debris flow and the positional change of the Electra in a six month period captured by the latter two aerial photos of the shipwreck and some four years of movement when one adds the 1938 blurry, enlarged photo, I conclude that the Electra, or what was eventually left of it, made its way into the channel leading to the lagoon and was subsequently swept into the lagoon where it or parts of it lie concealed by the silt and coral debris therein to this day.

Alternately, I propose that the Electra broke up, the lighter wings and other parts washed into the lagoon while the main fuselage section and nose kept working its way down the reef east and south until it washed off the reef many hundreds, possibly thousands of meters away.

This is why I believe that Robert Ballard found no airplane parts or aluminum during the August 2019 expedition as the special program, "Expedition Amelia" revealed. The target area where he spent a lot of time was way off to begin with if one believes what the aerial photos I've presented represent, and that the Electra traveled a great distance exceeding five football fields along the reef.

I hope that when Ballard returns to the island in 2022 or 2023 (due to delays caused by the pandemic) as an article suggested, and which he intimated during the broadcast, that he focuses not only on the beaches to the south and east of the shipwreck but also in the adjacent lagoon.

Exploring the latter will be an enormous task as the lagoon is a mile wide at its widest point. What may save time are "known" locations where natives say airplane debris washed up. Possibly, in the silt just offshore from these beaches, a major part of the plane or some aircraft aluminum will be found.

To paraphrase Ballard, *"One piece of her plane and we'll have the whole thing."*

Considering the anecdotal evidence of the Nikumaroro natives who found airplane parts washed up on lagoon beaches and used them to make implements, I believe it is highly likely that Robert Ballard would find "one part of her plane" in the lagoon—at least. The aerial photos and the enlargements I've presented do shout "airplane!" and do support and corroborate the one photo, the much-criticized landing wheel, upon which Ballard relied for this search.

Earlier, I mentioned that the mighty P&W "wasp" engines would have broken off just like the landing wheels obviously had just three months post-crashlanding per the 1937 Bevington photo. These airplane engines and landing wheels are very heavy objects and small for their compact weight. In 1937 on Ford Island one landing wheel broke off and the other is snapped and collapsed beneath the Electra fuselage. I've little doubt that the landing wheel seen in that 1937 photo probably broke off the aircraft last while it was subjected to surf and tide (after running out of fuel or the propeller no longer cleared the water).

How far would such heavy objects travel on the reef and at what daily speed? What if the other landing wheel and the engines remained attached to the fuselage and wing stubs? What if any of these objects is buried in one of those coral debris berms thrown up by storms? That's a smaller mystery still waiting to be solved. It's been nearly 85 years and counting. I do believe we will see discovery, soon.

Where are those airplane engines or what is left of them? I've constructed ¼ scale working models of this engine from the time I was 12 years old until recently. In 2007, I offered a DVD on eBay on how to successfully build this very difficult, fragile, and temperamental, working model engine from 1962. The basic parts and shapes of the wasp engine are well-known to me from counterweights to rocker arms to cylinder heads. Even broken off or broken apart those engine parts have unique shapes and might be easy to spot in a debris field. Locating that debris field is the very difficult part of the search especially in a lagoon that is very silty.

Yet, Robert Ballard found not one piece of aircraft aluminum in the ocean. Believe me, I was as surprised and possibly as disappointed as Robert Ballard was. My speculation is that the Electra continued its tidal dance and progress on the reef and went into the lagoon entrance. To this day, on the reef, in the entryway to the lagoon, visible in a recent aerial photo, there is a shiny, rectangular piece of debris which I believe to be aluminum and might possibly be a central fuselage remnant minus nose, tail, and wings. I wish that Ballard's people had flown their drone over it for a closer look.

Without knowing precisely how far past or south of the shipwreck Ballard searched underwater, one might speculate that the Electra did eventually fall off the reef. Ballard did remark that he wished to return to Nikumaroro and search the reef and beaches further south of the shipwreck.

Could it be, after all this time, that the engines, at least one of them, is still working its way south and east along the reef not having gone over the edge into much deeper water? Such a find that would turn out to be! Then, that engine and landing wheels may also be in the lagoon. The lagoon must be searched using a magnetometer arrangement with recovery of targets. No small task including getting equipment and support into the lagoon.

Turning to the question of what happened to Earhart and Noonan after their crash-landing on July 2, 1937 at Gardner / Nikumaroro, what I offer is mostly speculation. I admit that my speculation of their fates and being taken from the island by the Japanese is just that. I'm looking to make reasonable speculation, though. It is an interesting theory supported by many with many eyewitnesses swearing to the truth of what they saw.

If we accept as true that the last post-crash radio broadcast was made early on July 7, 1937 then we must assume that either the duo perished sometime in the next two days which is why the *Colorado* seaplanes saw no one signaling from the beaches, or that Earhart and Noonan were no longer on the island on July 9, 1937. And, sadly, one might also assume that the *Colorado* seaplane crews flew away too soon when they did not spot any aircraft, activity, or people.

It is also possible that either Earhart or Noonan or both were still alive during that seaplane flyby on July 9 but delirious from lack of water, illness, injuries, or from drinking saltwater from the lagoon or sea or from whatever apparatus they jury-rigged to try to make fresh water (evaporation and condensation for example). This conclusion leads to supporting the discovery (unearthing) of bones on the island by natives who informed Gallagher in 1940 they had buried the skull, and that those bones were in fact all that remained of the two castaways. The alternative conclusion is that the bones belong to a *Norwich City* crewman washed by the storm in November 1929 into the lagoon and deposited on a beach many kilometers to the south who survived for a short time and for some reason was either unaware or incapable of journeying back to the shipwreck and his shipmates waiting there to be rescued.

Now, have they found those same bones on Tarawa? The same bones Gallagher consigned to Suva, Fiji in 1940? I don't think so. The forensic people went through many boxes of bones and, per the National Geographic broadcast, only succeeded in finding a female skull in the last box they searched. How theatrical! It looked to me to be much more than a cranial remnant as described in 1940. It was remarked during the TV show that the natives of Tarawa save all unknown bones, but I find it incredible that there was only one female skull, and that that skull was located in the last box they searched. That scenario seems highly scripted and frankly doesn't ring true. My opinion does not make it untrue but judge for yourselves.

However, I could not ignore the competing idea and various theories that Earhart and Noonan were captured by the Japanese, nor could I ignore the 1939 statements in the National Archives about the mystery bottle found on a French beach in October of 1938.

The lengths someone took, a purported prisoner and forced labor crewman on a Japanese vessel, to toss a message in a small bottle off the coast of Spain in the hope of it reaching authorities complete with a tale of seeing Earhart in prison and containing what was represented as a lock of her hair, defy the conclusion that it was hoax.

Still, strange hoaxes have been created. The Piltdown Man hoax being one of the most elaborate, lasting for some forty years before the hoax was discovered. Then, another academic hoax embarrassed a professor: There, a professor was lured into finding and proclaiming new fossil discoveries only to later discover a piece of fossil evidence with his name on it!

Ha-ha!

Then, there is the hearsay evidence that well-known figures conversationally admitted or intimated that they knew the Japanese had imprisoned Earhart. The ultra-secret codebreaking of the Japanese codes does justify US Government silence and abandonment of Earhart and Noonan to their fates at the time. What is attributable to Admiral Nimitz circa 1960 about the Earhart disappearance is not definitive and unknown.

So, assuming the story that Earhart and Noonan were prisoners of the Japanese is true, coupled with my finding the Electra on the reef in those old aerial photos, it begs the question as to how they got off Gardner Island or Nikumaroro. Enter the 1935 photo purporting to show Earhart and Noonan on a dock on Jaluit except it was taken in 1935 before the circumnavigation flight. Then, one reads from the blogger's posted explanation which exposed the truth about the timeframe of the photo that the very ship in the photo is the *Koshu*, a naval survey vessel, towing a seaplane on a barge, *which took part in the search for Amelia Earhart in July 1937.*

Hence, in fairness to other theories, my conclusion that the only way to get the surviving duo from Gardner Island to Saipan via Jaluit is by using the *Koshu* (or another Japanese vessel participating in the search for the duo) as a rescue vessel (with a seaplane) which plucked Earhart and Noonan from Gardner island. The Japanese accused them of being spies based upon the contents of Earhart's briefcase, and then transported them to Japanese held territory aboard said "rescue" ship.

Adding to this collection of circumstantial evidence, if we assume that Robert Wallack was telling the truth and that he found Earhart's briefcase, passport, visas, and other papers in a briefcase locked in a safe on Saipan, then we must somehow connect or "get" that briefcase as well as Earhart and Noonan from Gardner Island to Jaluit Atoll (French message in a bottle) and then to Saipan. Those locations both have prisons.

The answer is and can only be the *Koshu* or possibly another Japanese Navy or fishing ship picked up the fliers. Here, we have to assume that the Japanese aboard the *Koshu* heard everything broadcast on July 2, 1937 and thereafter by Noonan and Earhart. Then, we must assume that the Japanese had intel gleaned from newspaper accounts and other means, possibly clandestine, possibly through their own radio direction-finders in Japan, and those onboard ship, and that they made a beeline to Gardner Island. A beeline which the Japanese populace who were listening on their shortwave radios clamored about having performed their own directional finding by tracing the signals back to the Phoenix Island chain.

Furthermore, we must assume that the *Koshu* or equivalent military ship was in the "vicinity" of Gardner Island such that the Japanese were able to sail and pull the fliers off the island before July 9 and the flyby of the seaplanes from the USS *Colorado*.

For my speculation to work, we have the believe that is exactly what the Japanese did. The flyers were on Gardner Island because their plane is there, its wreckage visible in the three to five photos discussed. If Earhart was spotted in Jaluit prison and gave a man a lock of her hair in a desperate attempt to tell the world that she was a prisoner, (later imprisoned on Saipan and executed), then we have to believe that it was the *Koshu* or another Japanese ship that picked up the fliers and sailed with them to the Marshall Islands.

To believe otherwise would require that the airplane images I found in those aerial photos were of another Electra, or so-called illusions cause by light and dark shadows which conveniently manifest as a Lockheed Electra in several photos taken at different times and of different locations by different camera operators around the shipwrecked *Norwich City*.

Hardly.

Earhart and Noonan certainly didn't swim, and they certainly didn't fly to Saipan, or construct a boat and sail there.

We further have to assume that the Japanese would have considered it a badge of their superiority and heroism in rescuing and returning Earhart and Noonan to America except they didn't. Why? They were hated spies!

Another question and assumption are therefore required to answer the above question: we have to assume that the briefcase belonging to Amelia Earhart was taken by her ashore on Gardner from the Electra; we must further assume, bearing in mind the 1939 intelligence report in the National Archives about the French nationals, that something or some things in that briefcase caused the Japanese rescuers' smiles to fade, and to treat the flyers as enemy spies.

Could some secret agenda contained in some correspondence or notes in her briefcase have sealed Earhart's and Noonan's fates within minutes of being picked up? Frankly, I cannot understand it any other way. If we assume that the Japanese scenario is true, something big and embarrassing in that briefcase, possibly even in their statements, changed friendliness and saving lives into grimaces and cold hearts for spies who might have information about the Japanese secret buildup of facilities, weapons, and their Navy in the Pacific. A secret the Japanese were intent on keeping secret at all costs.

We must recall that Japan attacked China on July 9, 1937 and that harsh words had been exchanged by the US and Japan. In the National Archives are pre-war reports about Japanese ships in the Pacific filed by passing boats, yachts, ships, and aircraft.

Intelligence was being collected by both sides, even from the yachting crowd judging by the circled words on the report in the National Archives about the French National who sailed too close to Mili Atoll, was arrested, but fortunately was released along with his American wife.

For the paranoid Japanese building battleships in secret and preparing for war in secret for over four years *before* Pearl Harbor, an innocuous note in her briefcase requesting that Earhart take notes and details of all Japanese ships she passed over in-flight (even her actual notes, themselves) would have angered the Japanese beyond any humanitarian thought of delivering the rescued castaways to the American searchers.

Then, was this "favor" and spying a *quid pro quo* for the construction of runways on Howland Island and for the availability of the crew and the Coast Guard ship *Itasca* plus fuel and supplies placed at Earhart's disposal? Remember the letter in the National Archives which Earhart wrote in 1936 to President Roosevelt asking for help in refueling in the Pacific? The one the president penciled in for his aides to *assist Mrs. Putnam*?

I can see that innocent-sounding request or *quid pro quo* being made by the President or Naval Intelligence to Amelia Earhart to report on observed Japanese ships and installations. Sounds innocent enough until you realize that to an enemy such as the Japanese at the time, that action is one which a spy performs.

Then, one can imagine the mind of the Japanese faced with the choice to either return or intern the duo after they plucked them off Gardner Island. We must assume the Japanese "knew" that the Electra had washed into deeper water, that Gardner Island was uninhabited, that no one observed the *Koshu* (or other Japanese ship) and the rescue.

At that moment, the Japanese were well-clear and steaming away with two spies. The Japanese must have realized they had perfect deniability where Earhart and Noonan were concerned and were no doubt smug that the great America would never see their female heroine (and spy) again.

Did the Japanese Ambassador in Washington, D.C. (Saito) know his government had Earhart on July 20, 1937 when that "grateful" note was acknowledged in his letter to Secretary of State Cordell Hull?

Under my speculative scenario, I believe he probably did.

I'm assuming that America did not tumble to the Japanese capturing Earhart until they decoded future messages or cracked JN-25 enough to read Japanese naval, coded messages about Earhart and Noonan and possibly their transfers from one ship or prison to another. Even by Midway in June of 1942, we still could not decode all Japanese messages.

At least by early 1939, the USA intelligence community and President Roosevelt had some idea of the "prisoner possibility" as raised by the mysterious message and lock of hair in the bottle found on a beach near Bordeaux, France in late 1938. That intelligence was secret and only declassified in 1977 (and then "lost" or misplaced for some four decades). Further corroboration of Earhart's capture and circumstances must have come from further decoded Japanese transmissions over time.

On the other hand, there is still a pending DNA analysis of the skull bones found on Tarawa. So far, not so good. It is alleged that these are the same bones found on Gardner Island in 1940 but, so far, there is no sign of proof of chain of custody. Regardless, the DNA was found not to be viable enough for analysis and still is to this day, August 2022.

One could easily assert that the skull came from Saipan and the unmarked grave of Earhart should DNA positively identify the skull as Amelia Earhart's. We will have to wait and see if viable DNA is found in future and then tested. So far, with the initial DNA test failure, no further results are forthcoming.

I did not allow this pending DNA analysis to deter me from writing this narrative in 2019. But now that the special expedition broadcast has aired this evening (October 20, 2019), I believe in the prisoner of the Japanese scenario (as a possible post-crash-aftermath) because I have evidence of the Electra on the reef at Gardner / Nikumaroro and it is one way to explain what happened to the fliers after July 7th and their last radio broadcast from the Electra.

I'll admit that I could be totally wrong about the prisoner of the Japanese aspect of my double-scenario and that the fliers did perish as castaways by a quirk of fate and because time ran out for them before they could run out onto the beach and wave to the circling *Colorado* seaplanes on July 9. Still, the Japanese quite probably could have also found them dead and took her briefcase as proof they located something of hers.

Remember, the penalty for a spy is severe and applies even to inept and bungling spies. The mere fact, if it could be proven, that Earhart had such a memo and had agreed to look for Japanese ships and fortifications while on-route to Howland Island, means that Earhart had *agreed to be a spy*.

Earhart probably didn't see it that way. It was a favor in return for the help offered by FDR to loan *Itasca* and crew, and to build runways on Howland Island for her. One country's patriot is another country's spy. If such a mission was offered to Earhart in exchange for the arrangements with *Itasca* and other US Navy assets, Earhart should have refused or at least divested herself of any compromising memos and avoided taking any notes during the flight even though it was mostly at night over those Japanese installations. Logically, an aircraft failure and ditching might put her in the hands of the Japanese. If the decision to report on Japanese ships and installations while on-route was made by Amelia Earhart, it was a foolish, naïve, and fateful decision.

Thus, are two competing "theories" joined together concerning the fate of Amelia Earhart and Fred Noonan from July 2, 1937 until her demise on Nikumaroro or by execution on Saipan. I believe the scenarios I've painted are each coherent and logical.

I have put a great deal of faith in a few documents and affidavits to piece together that reasonable speculation. Yes, some people lie for whatever reason but, as I suggested at the beginning of this narrative, *did everyone lie?*

In this short narrative, I admit that I have cherry-picked my witnesses and supporting information, and offered alternative thoughts, but I believe I've managed to get closer to the truth about where she crash-landed than anyone before me. Here, I salute Fred Hooven who initially posited, after much research into post-crash signals, that Earhart had crash-landed on Nikumaroro. He later rejected this idea. I mention Fred Hooven again because Ric Gillespie of TIGHAR did not originate the "Nikumaroro Hypothesis" except in name. Gillespie is criticized by many for never mentioning (true or not) Hooven whenever he speaks or writes about Amelia Earhart.

However, I do salute everyone who has worked on this mystery, and for the information I've gleaned online from various posts, excerpts, photos, discussions, and opinions.

I believe in what I see on those three aerial photos of the shipwrecked *Norwich City*, especially the June, 1941 photo which clearly shows the nose and fuselage of the Lockheed Electra. That is my anchor here, and my offer of proof that Earhart landed there on Gardner Island /Nikumaroro. It is a fixed point, so to speak, and from there flows the balance of my scenario with facts and arguments in support thereof.

Frankly, though perhaps pointless but speaks to my humanity, I hope Earhart and Noonan did perish on Nikumaroro instead of at the hands of the Japanese. This is my personal belief, a simple scenario: Earhart and Noonan landed, and quickly ran out of water ("...*can't last much longer*.") and were either incapable of responding to the Colorado seaplanes on July 9, or they were already dead. The island erased them quickly. I don't think they wandered too far from the north shore and the Norwich City while the Electra was still useful on the reef with a working engine for broadcasting up to July 7. Perhaps they thought that by venturing southward they might find water only to succumb under a ren tree.

I expect some of their remains or traces of their presence are still in the "coconut jungle" there on Nikumaroro along with Noonan's sextants and Amelia's briefcases (rotted away by now). That coconut jungle was their only potential source of water or coconut milk. For evidence, we have the story about the bones found in 1940 and Gallagher's impression that the remains found on Gardner/Nikumaroro might be of Amelia Earhart or so he wrote to his superiors at the time.

I hope that one day, the entire, verified truth will somehow be revealed. Hopefully, Robert Ballard will be successful in finding proof in the form of Electra aircraft wreckage in the lagoon at Nikumaroro in a 2022-3 expedition or thereafter. If so, then perhaps TIGHAR or some other organization will deem suitable a thorough search of the coconut jungle for their possible remains or other artifacts.

From an article by Caitlin Duan, *My Tribute to Amelia Earhart* (2020), below you will find the last known photograph taken of Amelia Earhart on July I, 1937 with Frank Howard whose oil company refueled her Lockheed Electra at Lae, New Guinea prior to Earhart's and Noonan's takeoff and disappearance on July 2, 1937.

And below, what started my journey was this photographic discovery from an aerial photo taken in June 1941 of the *Norwich City* wreck.

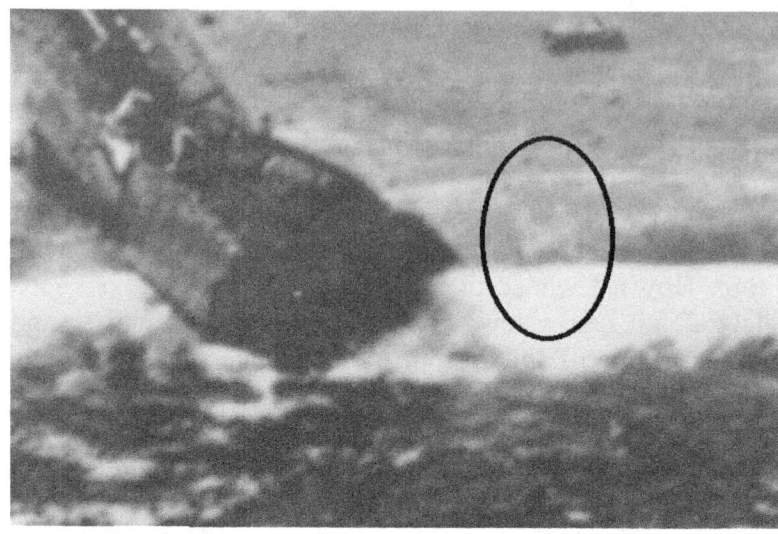

And the factory image that allowed me to see and recognize the Electra shape in the photographs.

I hope that you have enjoyed this armchair pursuit to determine the fate of Amelia Earhart and Fred Noonan, the new photographic evidence presented including the latter-day additions in this volume, and my speculating and combining competing theories about her disappearance into one theory based upon real documents and other facts.

My many thanks to my mother for providing me assistance with a superior education through New York University and Western New England University School of Law. Thanks to my sons, Jason and Justin, and to my daughter, Christina Avanesian, for your continued love and support. Many thanks to my wife Lori for her love, support, and enthusiasm for this work.

Then, I must express my love and gratitude to my three faithful companions, my lovely "Iggys" or Italian Greyhounds, Penne, Atia, and Augustus, who routinely begged me for cookies while I typed away if only to *selflessly* get the old man out of his chair, walking, and exercising!

"Daddy needs a walk!"

I do joke that I'm the fourth dog in this house, and that these three lovely creatures *adopted me.*

I invite you to leave a review of this work. Thank you. The adventure and these discoveries I've made await further expedition and a thorough search of the lagoon and southerly beaches and offshore at Nikumaroro. I hope to one day see proof in the form of airplane parts photographed or salvaged from the lagoon there. I'm presently awaiting to be interviewed on a *Chasing Amelia Earhart* podcast in August 2022. Such fun!

In memory of Amelia Earhart and Fred Noonan. Fate is the hunter. We'll find you, *eventually.*

Robert Grant Wealleans
Novato, CA
October 20, 2019

Made in the USA
Monee, IL
20 January 2023

25719979R00132